The Master Plan of Evangelism

presents a thorough examination of the Gospel accounts, revealing the objective of Christ's ministry and his strategy for carrying it out. Robert E. Coleman focuses on the underlying principles that consistently determined what Jesus' action would be in any given situation. By emulating his pattern, you'll be prepared to minister to the specific needs of those God brings into your life. This edition includes a study guide by Roy Fish, which contains thirteen lessons for applying Christ's principles for evangelism. With the help of *The Master Plan of Evangelism,* you can be sure that your course of action fits into God's overall plan for the Great Commission. Every Christian who seeks to follow and witness for Jesus Christ should read this significant and relevant book.

Books by Robert E. Coleman

Established by the Word
Introducing the Prayer Cell
Life in the Living Word
The Master Plan of Evangelism
The Spirit and the Word
Dry Bones Can Live Again
One Divine Moment (Editor)
Written in Blood
Evangelism in Perspective
They Meet the Master
The Mind of the Master
Songs of Heaven
Growing in the Word
The New Covenant
The Heartbeat of Evangelism
Evangelism on the Cutting Edge (Editor)
The Master Plan of Discipleship
The Spark That Ignites
Nothing to Do but to Save Souls
The Great Commission Lifestyle

Robert E. Coleman is director of the School of World Mission and Evangelism and Professor of Evangelism at Trinity Evangelical Divinity School in Deerfield, Illinois. He also directs the Institute of Evangelism at the Billy Graham Center in Wheaton, Illinois, and serves as dean of the International Schools of Evangelism.

Dr. Coleman is a founding member of the Lausanne Committee for World Evangelization, and a past president of the Academy for Evangelism in Theological Education. He is a graduate of Southwestern University, Asbury Theological Seminary, Princeton Theological Seminary, and received the Ph.D. from the University of Iowa.

He has written hundreds of articles and twenty books. Translations of one or more of his books are published, or are in the process of publication in ninety languages, with English editions alone approaching 5 million copies in print.

Words of Commendation

This little book has made an indelible mark on Christianity around the world. Published in 1963, it has been translated into scores of languages and touched the lives of millions through its simple biblical message.

To commemorate the thirtieth anniversary of its publication, Christian leaders have written their praise of this modern classic, reflecting on how it has touched their lives and ministries and how God has used it in shaping the course of discipleship and evangelism in the closing decades of this century.

To many of us who have a heart for evangelism Robert Coleman's book, *The Master Plan of Evangelism*, stands as a watershed resource on the subject. It has literally shaped the thinking of the evangelical community both in the United States and around the world on the subject of evangelism.

Time will only reveal the number of people who come to faith in Jesus Christ as a result of being released by Robert Coleman's book.

Joe C. Aldrich, president, Multnomah School of the Bible

Of all the books written on evangelism, this is a classic. If you want to impact your world on a personal level, this is one of the best tools you can find.

Ann Kiemel Anderson, author of *And with the Gift Came Laughter*

The needs and opportunities for world evangelism have seldom or ever been greater. *The Master Plan of Evangelism* has and is making a significant contribution to this effort. Any pastor or layperson who leads a group through the book and study guide will be well rewarded.

Congratulations on the 30th anniversary of publication. May the next thirty years see even greater interest and involvement in world evangelism.

Win Arn, Church Growth 2000

The Master Plan of Evangelism has enabled millions of Christians to more effectively share the good news of God's grace. In our day of the global village, of a pluralistic society, we need to find our direction from Jesus himself, for he is our mentor as well as our Redeemer.

Myron Augsburger, president,
Christian College Coalition

Dr. Robert Coleman is one of the most remarkable, effective exponents of evangelism of our time. He is a man of God, skilled in the art of teaching, preaching and applying discipleship. His book, *The Master Plan of Evangelism,* is already a classic and he is a legend in our time. This book is must reading for everyone who desires to be a disciple of the Lord Jesus Christ.

Bill Bright, founder and president,
Campus Crusade for Christ International

Robert Coleman's classic book reminds us all that the Lord Jesus was committed to make disciples who would then also make disciples and so on. It's a delightfully simple approach which the church today would do well to rediscover. It's effective too!

D. Stuart Briscoe, senior pastor, Elmbrook Church

This book is bold, brilliant and balanced. It is ideal for Christian workers.

Tony Campolo, author of *Wake Up, America!*

Outside of the Bible, I know of no book that has been more influential in shaping my life and ministry than *The Master Plan of Evangelism* . . . and I am proud to be the author's brother.

Lyman Coleman, president, Serendipity House

I first read *The Master Plan of Evangelism* nearly a decade and a half ago. This book transformed my idea of ministry and it helped me form a more biblical vision of Jesus Christ's Great Commission. This splendid work is required reading for students in my evangelism classes and I recommend it to everyone who wants to be a faithful disciple of Christ Jesus.

Lyle W. Dorsett, professor of educational ministries and evangelism, Wheaton College

Words of Commendation

The Master Plan of Evangelism is a true classic. Although first published in 1963, it is even more timely today as churches and evangelism movements unite in unprecedented ways for the task of seeing the Great Commission literally fulfilled in our generation. I recommend it to all believers with great delight.

>**Dick Eastman,** international president,
>Every Home for Christ

The Master Plan of Evangelism is a true classic of our time. Whenever I am asked by Christian leaders around the world for a source on the true meaning of discipleship, this book always is my first choice. Few books have had an equal impact over the centuries!

>**James F. Engle,** distinguished professor of
>marketing, research and strategy, Eastern College

The greatest insights are almost always simple. *The Master Plan of Evangelism* contains such insights. In it Robert Coleman has set forth an understanding of Jesus' approach to reaching out to precious people and invites us to do the same.

>**Richard J. Foster,** author of *Celebration of Discipline*

I have used *The Master Plan of Evangelism* in training student leaders and student workers for twenty-five years, and it remains a 'must read' on my list of recommendations for everyone engaged in discipleship. What makes Robert Coleman's treatment so different from other 'plans' of evangelism is that he has discerned from Scripture the heart of the Master as well as His methods.

>**Stephen A. Hayner,** president,
>InterVarsity Christian Fellowship

More than any other book, *The Master Plan of Evangelism* explains the method of Jesus and has informed my teaching on evangelism in the life of Jesus. Every serious student of evangelism must read this book, and every casual student of evangelism should begin here.

>**Joel D. Heck,** editor, *Evangelism*

No book on evangelical evangelism will invite sixty printings and press runs exceeding a million copies unless it has something urgently important to say. Readers of Coleman's *Master Plan of Evangelism* know the secret.

>**Carl F. H. Henry,** evangelical theologian and author

This little 'big book' is simple, hence profound. As expressing the life of Jesus of Nazareth, it translates readily into any culture. We have found it highly effective in our work in India and more recently in Eastern Europe. The combined edition of text and study guide is very useful. The book is a must for methodology since in the New Testament, God is the evangelist.

Samuel Kamaleson, vice president,
World Vision International

I first discovered *The Master Plan of Evangelism* while developing the training program for Youth for Christ, International staff workers. It has been the centerpiece ever since. I know of no single book on the methodology of evangelism that has more fidelity to the biblical pattern. This small book does more to help eager, highly motivated evangelists avoid the shortcuts and eventually harmful gimmicks of a modern, sales-oriented culture than anything I have found. Its widespread popularity and sales are evidence of a worldwide thrust from a biblically based method that goes beyond guilt, pressure techniques and Madison Avenue.

Jay Kesler, president, Taylor University

Coleman's book is a classic both in its New Testament theology and New Testament strategy.

Bruce Larson, co-pastor, The Crystal Cathedral

Robert Coleman's book might well be entitled *The Master's Plan for Evangelism.* By staying close to the Word and communicating the motivation of the Spirit, Coleman helps every Christian discover the simple joy of winning souls.

David L. McKenna, president,
Asbury Theological Seminary

This fine book was particularly strategic in my turning a corner in my own philosophy of ministry. After I got 'turned on' to it, I had our whole pastoral team of Lake Avenue Congregational Church read the book; then with plan and purpose we began discipling throughout the whole congregation. As a couple, Anne and I got new visions, too, for discipling in small groups, and have been doing it ever since.

Raymond C. Ortlund, president, Renewal Ministries;
president, Haven of Rest radio broadcast

I came across *The Master Plan of Evangelism* many years ago while serving as a missionary-evangelist in Latin America. When the Spanish-language version was published, I was honored to write the foreword to it for the sake of the tens of millions of Hispanic Christians in nearly twenty-five nations. Now that the thirtieth anniversary of the publication of Dr. Coleman's book is being celebrated, I join with the thousands of Christian leaders who have recommended it, used it, and seen the fruit of this New Testament master plan from the Master Himself.

> **Luis Palau,** president,
> Luis Palau Evangelistic Association

The Master Plan of Evangelism has been, to me, second only to the Bible in terms of how it has affected my life. Every six months I look to rekindle my fire and keep my focus by reading and rereading Mr. Coleman's book. In my library are usually two or three copies to pass on to people who I feel are truly serious about evangelism.

> **John M. Perkins,** president and publisher,
> *Urban Family* Magazine

The Master Plan of Evangelism has stimulated, instructed, and encouraged thousands of Christians around the world. This is because it is both biblical and practical. Robert Coleman's work will continue to bless God's people and be an instrument for building Christ's church.

> **Jim Reapsome,** editor, *Evangelical Missions Quarterly*

It is a great thing to be an evangelist who draws thousands to Jesus. It is an even greater thing to train thousands to be evangelists. That is exactly what Dr. Coleman has accomplished in his epochal presentation of Jesus as the Master "fisher-of-men.

> **Don Richardson,** author of *Peace Child* and *Eternity in Their Hearts*

The Master Plan of Evangelism is a classic—one of those books that occasionally comes along—that grips our attention, challenges our thinking and calls us to action. From my early days in Youth for Christ Robert Coleman's book has challenged me and countless Christians to share their faith in a way that brings honor to Christ.

> **Doug Ross,** executive director,
> Evangelical Christian Publishing Association

Evangelism is timeless. This book is timeless. I first read it twenty-eight years ago as a college student. It inspired me to take my faith to Chicago's inner-city black community and the tenement houses of the near west side; to live my faith among my fellow workers at my part-time job in Chicago's Loop. Robert Coleman's principles worked.

Recently, a member of a Bible class I was teaching said to me, 'Ruth, you know what one book has most profoundly affected my life? *The Master Plan of Evangelism*.' Robert Coleman's principles live on.

> **Ruth Senter,** senior staff writer, *Campus Life* Magazine

Clearly, Robert Coleman step by step gives the biblical mandate and how we can realize its fulfillment. I view this book as a must for every pastor as well as each follower of Christ.

> **George Sweeting,** chancellor, Moody Bible Institute

For many years I have used and recommended this excellent volume by Robert Coleman. I know of no more relevant book on discipleship that is based on Jesus' years of training the Twelve than this one. All who are interested in evangelism and the importance of mentoring will find *The Master Plan of Evangelism* insightful, useful, and helpful.

> **Chuck Swindoll,** pastor, author, radio Bible teacher

A rare privilege which very few human beings experience in their lifetime is a personal friendship with the author of a true literary classic. When my grandchildren's children read *The Master Plan of Evangelism*, I hope someone tells them that their great-grandfather knew and loved Robert Coleman and even called him 'Clem.'

> **C. Peter Wagner,** professor of church growth,
> Fuller Theological Seminary

The essence of the historic Navigator hallmark of multiplication is clearly taught in *The Master Plan of Evangelism*. It is must reading for every serious believer.

> **Dr. Jerry E. White,** international president,
> The Navigators

30TH ANNIVERSARY EDITION

The Master Plan of Evangelism

Robert E. Coleman

Foreword by Billy Graham

Introduction by Paul S. Rees
Study Guide by Roy J. Fish

Fleming H. Revell
A Division of Baker Book House
Grand Rapids, Michigan 49516

Library of Congress Cataloging-in-Publication Data

Coleman, Robert Emerson, 1928–
    The master plan of evangelism / Robert E. Coleman . foreword by Billy Graham ; with study guide by Roy J. Fish. — 30th anniversary ed.
    p.   cm.
    Includes bibliographical references.
    ISBN: 0-8007-5467-0
    1. Jesus Christ—Evangelistic methods. I. Fish, Roy J. II. Title.
BT590.E8C6   1993
269'.2—dc20   93-6792

The Master Plan of Evangelism © 1963, 1964, 1993
by Robert E. Coleman

Study Guide © 1972 by Fleming H. Revell Company,
a division of Baker Book House Company
P.O. Box 6287, Grand Rapids, Michigan 49516–6287

Printed in the United States of America

Unless otherwise noted, Scripture quotations are cited from the American Standard Revised Edition, © 1901 by Thomas Nelson & Sons.

Printing histories of English editions published in the Philippines, Singapore, and in India are not included; neither are histories of foreign language editions.

First published, January, 1963
2nd Printing, November 1964
3rd Printing, February, 1966
4th Printing, March, 1967
5th Printing, December, 1967
6th Printing, May, 1968
7th Printing, February, 1969
8th Printing, August, 1970
9th Printing, June, 1971
10th Printing, December, 1971
11th Printing, October, 1972
12th Printing, March, 1973
13th Printing, October, 1973
14th Printing, February, 1974
15th Printing, September, 1974
16th Printing, February, 1975
17th Printing, May, 1975
18th Printing, February, 1976
19th Printing, August, 1976
20th Printing, January, 1977
21st Printing, May, 1977
22nd Printing, December, 1977

23rd Printing, January, 1978
24th Printing, April, 1978
25th Printing, December, 1978
26th Printing, June, 1979
27th Printing, January, 1980
28th Printing, April, 1980
29th Printing, May, 1980
30th Printing, November, 1980
31st Printing, May, 1981
32nd Printing, December, 1982
33rd Printing, January, 1983
34th Printing, June, 1983
35th Printing, August, 1983
36th Printing, March, 1984
37th Printing, September, 1984
38th Printing, April, 1985
39th Printing, December, 1985
40th Printing, March, 1986
41st Printing, June, 1986
42nd Printing, September, 1986
43rd Printing, January, 1987
44th Printing, January, 1987

45th Printing, February, 1987
46th Printing, August, 1987
47th Printing, January, 1988
48th Printing, May, 1988
49th Printing, August, 1988
50th Printing, April, 1989
51st Printing, June, 1989
52nd Printing, November, 1989
53rd Printing, January, 1990
54th Printing, August, 1990
55th Printing, January, 1991
56th Printing, March, 1991
57th Printing, August, 1991
58th Printing, October, 1991
59th Printing, January, 1992
60th Printing, March, 1992
61st Printing, August, 1992
62nd Printing, November, 1992
63rd Printing, February, 1993
64th Printing, May 1993
65th Printing, April 1994

To
LYMAN and MARGARET
who dared to follow
the Master plan

Contents

Foreword

Few books have had as great an impact on the cause of world evangelization in our generation as Robert Coleman's *The Master Plan of Evangelism*. For thirty years this classic study has challenged and instructed untold numbers of individuals in reaching our world for Christ. I am delighted it now has been reprinted in this special thirtieth anniversary edition.

The secret of this book's impact is not hard to discover. Instead of drawing on the latest popular fad or newest selling technique, Dr. Coleman has gone back to the Bible and has asked one critical question: What was Christ's strategy of evangelism? In so doing, he has pointed us to the unchanging, simple (and yet profound) biblical principles which must undergird any authentic evangelistic outreach.

For that reason there is a timeless quality to this book, and just as it has spoken to men and women for three decades, so it now deserves to be discovered afresh by a new generation of Christians who have glimpsed the heartbeat of their Lord for evangelism.

May God continue to use this book to call each of us to God's priority for his people—the priority to reach out in love to a confused and dying world with the good news of God's forgiveness and peace and hope through Jesus Christ.

Billy Graham

15

Introduction

"Philosophers," wrote Karl Marx, "have only *interpreted* the world differently; the point is, however, to *change* it."

However unlike they are in fundamental affirmations, the Christian gospel and communism are at this point in agreement. But the agreement goes little further. Distinctively, the Church proclaims the changed world as the consequence of changed men. Reflective man produces new philosophies; it is only regenerate man who holds the clue to a society that is really new.

It is the conviction, grounded in the good news that "God was in Christ, reconciling the world unto Himself," that makes evangelism immensely more than a theory or a slogan. It brings it into focus as a necessity.

At this point, however, the question rises: How do we go forward with an evangelism—a widening of the circle of faith so that it includes more and more people who have transformingly trusted Christ as Savior—that is continuous, contagious, and compelling?

Robert E. Coleman has presented a set of principles and sketched a scheme which, studied carefully, will go far toward rescuing the concept of evangelism from the realm of the "special" and the "occasional," and anchoring where it belongs in the essential, ongoing life and witness of the congregation.

There is nothing in the following pages that belittles what the Spirit of God has done, and continues to do, through the colossal, concerted, temporary undertakings of such evangelistic specialists as Moody, Sunday, or Graham. On the other hand, there is much that beckons us to the disciple-winning that works through small groups and builds toward congregational witness—all of it calculated to demonstrate the connection between the Gospel to which we bear testimony and the life which that Gospel enables us to live.

The author's work, concentrating as it does on the pattern we see in our Lord and his disciples, is saturated with Scripture. His style is unembellished. It is plain. It is direct. It unfailingly echoes the transparent sincerity of the mind that has thought long on the theme with which it is at grips.

Only this morning I heard a radio speaker make the observation that, in most matters, we move in either of two directions: from *words* to *things*, or from *things* to *words*. That is to say, if we do not make the journey from theories and ideals to concrete situations, then the concrete situations will be lost under a smog of words.

From the latter peril I believe this earnest volume can help deliver us. It is therefore a pleasure to commend it.

Paul S. Rees

I am the way
John 14:6

Preface
The Master and His Plan

The Problem in Evangelistic Methods

Objective and relevance—these are the crucial issues of our work. Both are interrelated, and the measure by which they are made compatible will largely determine the significance of all our activity. Merely because we are busy, or even skilled, doing something does not necessarily mean that we are getting anything accomplished. The question must always be asked: Is it worth doing? And does it get the job done?

This is a question that should be posed continually in relation to the evangelistic activity of the church. Are our efforts to keep things going fulfilling the great commission of Christ? Do we see an ever-expanding company of dedicated people reaching the world with the gospel as a result of our ministry? That we are busy in the church trying to work one program of evangelism after another cannot be denied. But are we accomplishing our objective?

19

Form Follows Function

Concern at this point immediately focuses the need for a well-thought-through strategy of movement day by day in terms of the long-range goal. We must know how a course of action fits into the overall plan God has for our lives if it is to thrill our souls with a sense of destiny. This is true of any particular procedure or technique employed to propagate the gospel. Just as a building is constructed according to the plan for its use, so everything we do must have a purpose. Otherwise our activity can be lost in aimlessness and confusion.

A Study in Principles

That is why this study has been attempted. It is an effort to see controlling principles governing the movements of the Master in the hope that our own labors might be conformed to a similar pattern. As such, the book does not seek to interpret specific methods of Jesus in personal or mass evangelism.[1] Rather this is a study in principles underlying his ministry—principles which determined his methods. One might call it a study in his strategy of evangelism around which his life was oriented while he walked on the earth.

More Research Needed

There has been surprisingly little published along this line, though, of course, most books dealing with evangelistic methods will have something to say about it in passing. The same could be said for studies in Jesus' teaching methods,[2] as well as the general histories treating the life and work of Christ.[3]

Probably the most careful study to date in the Master's larger plan of evangelism has been done in reference to the training of the disciples, of which A. B. Bruce's *The Training of the Twelve* is the best.[4] First published in 1871 and revised in 1899, this narrative of the disciples' growth in the presence of the Master is still unsurpassed for wealth of insights into this subject. Another volume, *Pastor Pastorum* by Henry Latham, written in 1890, gives particular attention to Jesus' way of training men, though less comprehensive in its analysis.[5] Since the time of these earlier studies a number of other smaller volumes have appeared which offer helpful stimulus in pursuing this theme.[6] Not all of these works have the same evangelical theological viewpoint, but it is interesting to note that they come out at about the same place when it comes to evaluating the central thrust of Jesus' work with the disciples.

This is likewise true of numerous practical works on various phases of the church life and ministry which have been published in recent years, most notably in the literature pertaining to the growing small group and lay witness movement in the church. While aware that these authors have not written primarily from the standpoint of evangelistic strategy, we must acknowledge our indebtedness to them for their reckoning of fundamental principles in the ministry and mission of our Lord.

However, the subject of Jesus' basic strategy has rarely been given the attention it deserves. Though we are appreciative of the labors of those who have considered it, and are not unmindful of their findings, the need for further investigation and clarification is always with us, and this is especially true of study within the primary sources themselves.

Our Plan of Study

One has to go to the New Testament, and the Gospels in particular, to really see the plan of Jesus. They are after all the only eyewitness accounts that we have of the Master at work (Luke 1:2, 3; John 20:30; 21:24; 1 John 1:1). To be sure, the Gospels were written primarily to show us Christ, the Son of God, and that by faith we can have life in his name (John 20:31). But what sometimes we fail to realize is that the revelation of that life in Christ includes the way he lived and taught others so to live. We must remember that the witnesses who wrote the books not only saw the truth; they were changed by it. For this reason, in telling the story they invariably bring out those things which influenced them and others to leave all that they had to follow the Master. Not everything is reported, of course. Like any historical narrator, the Gospel writers paint a picture of the whole by elaborating upon a few characteristic persons and experiences, while bringing out certain critical points in the development of events. But of those things which are carefully selected and recorded in absolute integrity under the inspiration of the Holy Spirit, we can be sure that they are intended to teach us how to follow in the way of the Master. That is why the scriptural accounts of Jesus constitute our best, and only inerrant, Textbook on Evangelism.

Hence the plan of this study has been to trace the steps of Christ as portrayed in the Gospels without undue recourse to secondary materials. In this pursuit, the inspired account of his life and work has been examined many times and from many angles trying to discover a motivating reason for the way he went about his mission. His tactics have been analyzed from the standpoint of his ministry as a whole, hoping thereby to see the larger meaning of his methods with people. Admittedly the task has not been easy, and I would be the first to acknowledge that there is more to learn. The boundless dimensions of the Lord of Glory simply cannot be confined within any human interpretation of his perfection, and the longer one looks at him, the more one sees this to be the case.

Christ, a Perfect Example

Yet recognizing this fact, there is no study more rewarding. Limited as our faculties of perception may be, we know that in the Master we have a perfect Teacher. He never made a mistake. Though partaking of our life, and being tempted in all points as we are, he was not bound by the limitations of the flesh which he accepted for our sake. Even when he chose not to exercise his divine omniscience, his mind was clear. He always knew what was right, and as the perfect Man, he lived as God would live among humans.

His Objective Was Clear

The days of his flesh were but the unfolding in time of the plan of God from the beginning. It was always before his mind. He intended to save out of the world a people for himself and to build a church of the Spirit which would never perish. He had his sights on the day his Kingdom would come in glory and in power. This world was his by creation, but he did not seek to make it his permanent abiding place. His mansions were in the sky. He was going to prepare a place for his people that had foundations eternal in the heavens.

No one was excluded from his precious purpose. His love was universal. Make no mistake about it. He was "the Saviour of the world" (John 4:42). God wanted all men to be saved and to come to a knowledge of the truth. To that end Jesus gave himself to provide a salvation from all sin for all men. In that he died for one, he died for all. Contrary to our superficial thinking, there never was a distinction in his mind between home and foreign missions. To Jesus it was all world evangelism.

He Planned to Win

His life was ordered by his objective. Everything he did and said was a part of the whole pattern. It had significance because it contributed to the ultimate purpose of his life in redeeming the world for God. This was the motivating vision governing his behavior. His steps were ordered by it. Mark it well. Not for one moment did Jesus lose sight of his goal.

That is why it is so important to observe the way Jesus maneuvered to achieve his objective. The Master disclosed God's strategy of world conquest. He had confidence in the future precisely because he lived according to that plan in the present. There was nothing haphazard about his life—no wasted energy, not an idle word. He was on business for God (Luke 2:49). He lived, he died, and he rose again according to schedule. Like a general plotting his course of battle, the Son of God calculated to win. He could not afford to take a chance. Weighing every alternative and variable factor in human experience, he conceived a plan that would not fail.

Worth Careful Consideration

It is tremendously revealing to study it. Serious reflection at this point will bring the student of Christ to some profound and perhaps shattering conclusions, though the realization will likely be slow and arduous. In fact, at first glance it might even appear that Jesus had no plan. Another approach might discover some particular technique but miss the underlying pattern of it all. This is one of the marvels of his strategy. It is so unassuming and silent that it is unnoticed by the hurried churchman. But when the realization of his controlling method finally dawns on the open mind of the disciple he will be amazed at its simplicity and wonder how he could have ever failed to see it before. Nevertheless, when his plan is reflected on, the basic philosophy is so different from that of the modern church that its implications are nothing less than revolutionary.

The following pages attempt to clarify eight guiding principles of the Master's plan. However, it must be said that the steps are not to be understood as invariably coming in this sequence, as if the last were not initiated until the others had been mastered. Actually all of the steps were implied in each one, and in some degree they all began with the first. The outline is intended only to give structure to his method and to bring out the progressive logic of the plan. We will observe that as the ministry of Jesus Christ develops, the steps become more pronounced and the sequence more discernible.

He chose from them twelve
Luke 6:13

1

Selection

Men Were His Method

It all started by Jesus calling a few men to follow him. This revealed immediately the direction his evangelistic strategy would take. His concern was not with programs to reach the multitudes, but with men whom the multitudes would follow. Remarkable as it may seem, Jesus started to gather these men before he ever organized an evangelistic campaign or even preached a sermon in public. Men were to be his method of winning the world to God.

The initial objective of Jesus' plan was to enlist men who could bear witness to his life and carry on his work after he returned to the Father. John and Andrew were the first to be invited as Jesus left the scene of the great revival of the Baptist at Bethany beyond the Jordan (John 1:35–40). Andrew in turn brought his brother Peter (John 1:41, 42). The next day Jesus found Philip on his way to Galilee, and Philip found Nathaniel (John 1:43–51). There is no evidence of haste in the selection of these disciples, just determination. James,

27

the brother of John, is not mentioned as one of the group until the four fishermen are recalled several months later by the Sea of Galilee (Mark 1:19; Matt. 4:21). Shortly afterward Matthew is called to follow the Master as Jesus passed through Capernaum (Mark 2:13, 14; Matt. 9:9; Luke 5:27, 28). The particulars surrounding the call of the other disciples are not recorded in the Gospels, but it is believed that they all occurred in the first year of the Lord's ministry.[1]

As one might expect these early efforts of soul winning had little or no immediate effect upon the religious life of his day, but that did not matter greatly. For as it turned out, these few early converts of the Lord were destined to become the leaders of his church that was to go with the gospel to the whole world, and from the standpoint of his ultimate purpose, the significance of their lives would be felt throughout eternity. That's the only thing that counts.

Men Willing to Learn

What is more revealing about these men is that at first they do not impress us as being key men. None of them occupied prominent places in the synagogue, nor did any of them belong to the Levitical priesthood. For the most part they were common laboring men, probably having no professional training beyond the rudiments of knowledge necessary for their vocation. Perhaps a few of them came from families of some considerable means, such as the sons of Zebedee, but none of them could have been considered wealthy. They had no academic degrees in the arts and philosophies of their day. Like their Master, their formal education likely consisted only of the synagogue schools. Most of them were raised in the poor section of the country around Galilee. Apparently the only one of the twelve who came from the more refined region of Judea was Judas Iscariot. By any standard of sophisticated culture then and now they would surely be considered as a rather ragged collection of souls. One might wonder how Jesus could ever use them. They were impulsive, temperamental, easily offended, and had all the prejudices of their environment. In short, these men selected by the Lord to be his assistants represented an average cross section of society in their day.[2] Not the kind of group one would expect to win the world for Christ.

Yet Jesus saw in these simple men the potential of leadership for the Kingdom. They were indeed "unlearned and ignorant" according to the world's standard (Acts 4:13), but they were teachable. Though often mistaken in their judgments and slow to comprehend spiritual things, they were honest men, willing to confess their need. Their mannerisms may have been awkward and their abilities limited, but with the exception of the traitor, their hearts were big. What is perhaps most significant about them was their sincere yearning for God and the realities of his life. The superficiality of the religious life about them had not obsessed their hope for the Messiah (John 1:41, 45, 49; 6:69). They were fed up with the hypocrisy of the ruling aristocracy. Some of them had already joined the revival movement of John the Baptist (John 1:35). These men were looking for someone to lead them in the way of salvation. Such men, pliable in the hands of the Master, could be molded into a new image—Jesus can use anyone who wants to be used.

Concentrated on a Few

In noting this fact, however, one does not want to miss the practical truth of how Jesus did it. Here is the wisdom of his method, and in observing it, we return again to the fundamental principle of concentration on those he intended to use. One cannot transform a world except as individuals in the world are transformed, and individuals cannot be changed except as they are molded in the hands of the Master. The necessity is apparent not only to select a few helpers, but also to keep the group small enough to be able to work effectively with them.

Hence, as the company of followers around Jesus increased, it became necessary by the middle of his second year of ministry to narrow the select company to a more manageable number. Accordingly Jesus "called his disciples, and he chose from them twelve, whom also he named apostles" (Luke 6:13–17; cf., Mark 3:13–19). Regardless of the symbolical meaning one prefers to put on the number twelve,[3] it is clear that Jesus intended these men to have unique privileges and responsibilities in the Kingdom work.

This does not mean that Jesus' decision to have twelve apostles excluded others from following him, for as we know, many more were numbered among his associates, and some of these became very effective workers in the church. The seventy (Luke 10:1); Mark, the Gospel writer; James, his own brother (1 Cor. 15:7; Gal. 2:9, 12; cf., John 2:12 and 7:2–10), are notable examples of this. Nevertheless, we must acknowledge that there was a rapidly diminishing priority given to those outside the Twelve.

The same rule could be applied in reverse, for within the select apostolic group Peter, James, and John seemed to enjoy a more special relationship to the Master than did the other nine. Only these privileged few are invited into the sick room of Jairus's daughter (Mark 5:37; Luke 8:51); they alone go up with the Master and behold his glory on the Mount of Transfiguration (Mark 9:2; Matt. 17:1; Luke 9:28); and amid the olive trees of Gethsemane casting their ominous shadows in the light of the full Passover moon, these members of the inner circle waited nearest to their Lord while he prayed (Mark 14:33; Matt. 26:37). So noticeable is the preference given to these three that had it not been for the incarnation of selflessness in the person of Christ, it could well have precipitated feelings of resentment on the part of the other apostles. The fact that there is no record of the disciples complaining about the preeminence of the three, though they did murmur about other things, is proof that where preference is shown in the right spirit and for the right reason offense need not arise.[4]

The Principle Observed

All of this certainly impresses one with the deliberate way that Jesus proportioned his life to those he wanted to train. It also graphically illustrates a fundamental principle of teaching: that other things being equal, the more concentrated the size of the group being taught, the greater the opportunity for effective instruction.[5]

Jesus devoted most of his remaining life on earth to these few disciples. He literally staked his whole ministry on them. The world could be indifferent toward him and still not defeat his strategy. It even caused him no great concern when his followers on the fringes of things gave up their allegiance when confronted with the true meaning of the Kingdom (John 6:66). But he could not bear to have his close disciples miss his purpose. They had to understand the truth and be sanctified by it (John 17:17), else all would be lost. Thus he prayed "not for the world," but for the few God gave him "out of the world" (John 17:6, 9).[6] Everything depended on their faithfulness if the world would believe in him "through their word" (John 17:20).

Not Neglecting the Masses

It would be wrong, however, to assume on the basis of what has here been emphasized that Jesus neglected the masses. Such was not the case. Jesus did all that any man could be asked to do and more to reach the multitudes. The first thing he did when he started his ministry was to identify himself boldly with the great mass revival movement of his day by baptism at the hands of John (Mark 1:9–11; Matt. 3:13–17; Luke 3:21, 22), and he later went out of his way to praise this work of the great prophet (Matt. 11:7–15; Luke 7:24–28). He continuously preached to the crowds that followed his miracle-working ministry. He taught them. He fed them when they were hungry. He healed their sick and cast out demons among them. He blessed their children. Sometimes the whole day would be spent ministering to their needs, even to the extent that he had "no leisure so much as to eat" (Mark 6:31). In every way possible Jesus manifested to the masses of humanity a genuine concern. These were the people that he came to save—he loved them, wept over them, and finally died to save them from their sin. No one could think that Jesus shirked mass evangelism.

Multitudes Aroused

In fact, the ability of Jesus to impress the multitudes created a serious problem in his ministry. He was so successful in expressing to them his compassion and power that they once wanted "to take him by force, to make him King" (John 6:15). One report by the followers of John the Baptist said that "all men" were clamoring for his attention (John 3:26). Even the Pharisees admitted among themselves that the world had gone after him (John 12:19), and bitter as the admission must have been, the chief priests concurred in this opinion (John 11:47, 48). However one looks at it, the Gospel record certainly does not indicate that Jesus lacked any popular following among the masses, despite their hesitating loyalty, and this condition lasted to the end. Indeed, it was the fear of this friendly mass feeling for Jesus that prompted his accusers to capture him in the absence of the people (Mark 12:12; Matt. 21:26; Luke 20:19).

Had Jesus given any encouragement to this popular sentiment among the masses, he easily could have had all the kingdoms of the world at his feet. All he had to do was to satisfy the temporal appetites and curiosities of the people by his supernatural power. Such was the temptation presented by Satan in the wilderness when Jesus was urged to turn stones into bread and to cast himself down from a pinnacle of the temple that God might bear him up (Matt. 4:1–7; Luke 4:1–4, 9–13). These spectacular things would surely have excited the applause of the crowd. Satan was not offering Jesus anything when he promised him all the kingdoms of the world if the Master would only worship him (Matt. 4:8–10). The arch-deceiver of men knew full well that Jesus automatically would have this if he just turned his concentration from the things that mattered in the eternal Kingdom.[7]

But Jesus would not play to the galleries. Quite the contrary. Repeatedly he took special pains to allay the superficial popular support of the multitudes which had been occasioned by his extraordinary power (e.g., John 2:23–3:3; 6:26, 27). Frequently he would even ask those who were the recipients of his healing to say nothing about it to prevent mass demonstrations by the easily aroused multitudes.[8] Likewise, with the disciples following his transfiguration on the Mount "He charged them that they should tell no man what things they had seen" until after his resurrection (Mark 9:9; Matt. 17:9). On other occasions when applauded by the crowd, Jesus would slip away with his disciples and go elsewhere to continue his ministry.[9]

His practice in this respect sometimes rather annoyed his followers who did not understand his strategy. Even his own brothers and sisters, who yet did not believe in him, urged him to abandon this policy and make an open show of himself to the world, but he refused to take their advice (John 7:2–9).

Few Seemed to Understand

In view of this policy, it is not surprising to note that few people were actually converted during the ministry of Christ, that is, in any clearcut way. Of course, many of the multitudes believed in Christ in the sense that his divine ministry was acceptable,[10] but comparatively few seemed to have grasped the meaning of the gospel. Perhaps his total number of devoted followers at the end of his earthly ministry numbered little more than the five hundred brethren to whom Jesus appeared after the resurrection (1 Cor. 15:6), and only about 120 tarried in Jerusalem to receive the baptism of the Holy Spirit (Acts 1:15). Though this number is not small considering that his active ministry extended only over a period of three years, yet if at this point one were to measure the effectiveness of his evangelism by the number of his converts, Jesus doubtless would not be considered among the most productive mass evangelists of the church.

His Strategy

Why? Why did Jesus deliberately concentrate his life on comparatively so few people? Had he not come to save the world? With the glowing announcement of John the Baptist ringing in the ears of multitudes, the Master easily could have had an immediate following of thousands if he wanted them. Why did he not then capitalize on his opportunities to enlist a mighty army of believers to take the world by storm? Surely the Son of God could have adopted a more enticing program of mass recruitment. Is it not rather disappointing that one with all the powers of the universe at his command would live and die to save the world, yet in the end have only a few ragged disciples to show for his labors?

The answer to this question focuses at once on the real purpose of his plan for evangelism. Jesus was not trying to impress the crowd, but to usher in a kingdom. This meant that he needed people who could lead the multitudes. What good would it have been for his ultimate objective to arouse the masses to follow him if these people had no subsequent supervision or instruction in the Way? It had been demonstrated on numerous occasions that the crowd was an easy prey to false gods when left without proper care. The masses were like helpless sheep wandering aimlessly without a shepherd (Mark 6:34; Matt. 9:36; 14:14). They were willing to follow almost anyone who came along with some promise for their welfare, be it friend or foe. That was the tragedy of the hour—the noble aspirations of the people were easily excited by Jesus, but just as quickly thwarted by the deceitful religious authorities who controlled them. The spiritually blind leaders of Israel (John 8:44; 9:39–41; 12:40; cf., Matt. 23:1–39), though comparatively few in number,[11] completely dominated the affairs of the people. For this reason, unless Jesus' converts were given competent men of God to lead them on and protect them in the truth they would soon fall into confusion and despair, and the last state would be worse than the first. Thus, before the world could ever be permanently helped, people would have to be raised up who could lead the multitudes in the things of God.

Jesus was a realist. He fully realized the fickleness of depraved human nature as well as the satanic forces of this world amassed against humanity, and in this knowledge he based his evangelism on a plan that would meet the need. The multitudes of discordant and bewildered souls were potentially ready to follow him, but Jesus individually could not possibly give them the personal care they needed. His only hope was to get leaders inspired by his life who would do it for him. Hence, he concentrated on those who were to be the beginning of this leadership. Though he did what he could to help the multitudes, he had to devote himself primarily to a few men, rather than the masses, so that the masses could at last be saved. This was the genius of his strategy.

The Principle Applied Today

Yet, strangely enough, it is scarcely comprehended in practice today. Most of the evangelistic efforts of the church begin with the multitudes under the assumption that the church is qualified to preserve what good is done. The result is our spectacular emphasis on numbers of converts, candidates for baptism, and more members for the church, with little or no genuine concern manifested toward the establishment of these souls in the love and power of God, let alone the preservation and continuation of the work.

Surely if the pattern of Jesus at this point means anything at all, it teaches that the first duty of a church leadership is to see to it that a foundation is laid in the beginning on which can be built an effective and continuing evangelistic ministry to the multitudes. This will require more concentration of time and talents on fewer people in the church while not neglecting the passion for the world. It will mean raising up trained disciplers "for the work of ministering" with the pastor and church staff (Eph. 4:12).[12] A few people so dedicated in time will shake the world for God. Victory is never won by the multitudes.

Some might object to this principle when practiced by the Christian worker on the ground that favoritism is shown toward a select group in the church. But be that as it may, it is still the way that Jesus concentrated his life, and it is necessary if any lasting leadership is to be trained. Where it is practiced out of a genuine love for the whole church, and due concern is manifested toward the needs of the people, objections can at least be reconciled to the mission being accomplished. However, the ultimate goal must be clear to the worker, and there can be no hint of selfish partiality displayed in relationships to all. Everything that is done with the few is for the salvation of the multitudes.

Modern Demonstrations

This principle of selectivity and concentration is engraved in the universe, and will bring results no matter who practices it, whether or not the church believes it. Look at any successful leadership training program in business, industry, government, or the military.

On a global scale, it is surely not without significance that the early leaders of communism, always alert to what works, adopted in a large measure this method of the Lord as their own.[13] Using it to their own devious end they have multiplied from a handful of zealots to a vast conspiracy of followers that until recently enslaved nearly half the people of the world. They are a modern-day example of what Jesus demonstrated so clearly in his day that the multitudes can be won easily if they are just given leaders to follow.[14]

Time for Action

It is time that the church realistically face the situation. Our days of trifling are running out. The evangelistic program of the church has bogged down on nearly every front, especially across the affluent Western world. In many lands the enfeebled church is not even keeping up with the exploding population. All the while the satanic forces of this world are becoming more relentless and brazen in their attack. It is ironic when one stops to think about it. In an age when facilities for rapid communication of the gospel are available to the church as never before, there are actually more unevangelized people on the earth today than before the invention of the horseless carriage.[15]

Yet in appraising the tragic condition of affairs today, we must not become frantic in trying to reverse the trend overnight. Perhaps that has been our problem. In our concern to stem the tide, we have launched one crash program after another to reach the multitudes with the saving Word of God. But what we have failed to comprehend in our frustration is that the real problem is not with the masses—what they believe, how they are governed, whether they are fed a wholesome diet or not. All these things considered so vital are ultimately manipulated by others, and for this reason, before we can resolve the exploitation of the people we must get to those whom the people follow.

This, of course, puts a priority on winning and training those already in responsible positions of leadership. But if we can't begin at the top, then let us begin where we are and train a few of the lowly to become the great. And let us remember, too, that one does not have to have the prestige of the world to be greatly used in the Kingdom of God. Anyone who is willing to follow Christ can become a mighty influence on the world providing, of course, this person has the proper training.

Here is where we must begin just like Jesus. It will be slow, tedious, painful, and probably unnoticed by people at first, but the end result will be glorious, even if we don't live to see it. Seen this way, though, it becomes a big decision in the ministry. We must decide where we want our ministry to count—in the momentary applause of popular recognition or in the reproduction of our lives in a few chosen people who will carry on our work after we have gone. Really it is a question of which generation we are living for.

But we must go on. It is necessary now to see how Jesus trained his men to carry on his work. The whole pattern is part of the same method, and we cannot separate one phase from the other without destroying its effectiveness.

Lo, I am with you always
Matthew 28:20

2

Association

He Stayed with Them

Having called his men, Jesus made a practice of being with them. This was the essence of his training program—just letting his disciples follow him.

When one stops to think of it, this was an incredibly simple way of doing it. Jesus had no formal school, no seminaries, no outlined course of study, no periodic membership classes in which he enrolled his followers. None of these highly organized procedures considered so necessary today entered into his ministry. Amazing as it may seem, all Jesus did to teach these men his way was to draw them close to himself. He was his own school and curriculum.

The natural informality of this teaching method of Jesus stood in striking contrast to the formal, almost scholastic procedures of the scribes. These religious teachers insisted on their disciples adhering strictly to certain rituals and formulas of knowledge which distinguished them from others; whereas Jesus asked only that his disciples follow him. Knowledge was not communicated by the Master in terms of laws and dogmas, but in the living personality of One who walked among them. His disciples were distinguished, not by outward conformity to certain rituals, but by being with him, and thereby participating in his doctrine (John 18:19).

To Know Was to Be With

It was by virtue of this fellowship that the disciples were permitted "to know the mysteries of the Kingdom of God" (Luke 8:10). Knowledge was gained by association before it was understood by explanation. This was best expressed when one of the band asked, "How know we the way?" reflecting his frustration at the thought of the holy trinity. Jesus replied: "I am the way, the truth, and the life" (John 14:5, 6), which was to say that the point in question already was answered, if the disciples would but open their eyes to the spiritual reality incarnated in their midst.

This simple methodology was revealed from the beginning by the invitation that Jesus gave to the men he wanted to lead. John and Andrew were invited to "come and see" the place where Jesus stayed (John 1:39). Nothing more was said. Yet what more needed to be said? At home with Jesus they could talk things over and there in private see intimately into his nature and work. Philip was addressed in the same essential manner, "Follow me" (John 1:43). Evidently impressed by this simple approach, Philip invited Nathaniel also to "come and see" the Master (John 1:46). One living sermon is worth a hundred explanations. Later when James, John, Peter, and Andrew were found mending their nets, Jesus used the same familiar words, "Come ye after me," only this time adding the reason for it, "and I will make you fishers of men" (Mark 1:17; cf., Matt. 4:19; Luke 5:10). Likewise, Matthew was called from the tax collector's booth with the same invitation, "Follow me" (Mark 2:14; Matt. 9:9; Luke 5:27).

The Principle Observed

See the tremendous strategy of it. By responding to this initial call believers in effect enrolled themselves in the Master's school where their understanding could be enlarged and their faith established. There were certainly many things which these men did not understand—things which they themselves freely acknowledged as they walked with him; but all these problems could be dealt with as they followed Jesus. In his presence they could learn all that they needed to know.

This principle which was implied from the start was given specific articulation later when Jesus chose from the larger group about him the Twelve "that they might be with him" (Mark 3:14; cf., Luke 6:13). He added, of course, that he was going to send them forth "to preach, and to have authority to cast out devils," but often we fail to realize what came first. Jesus made it clear that before these men were "to preach" or "to cast out devils" they were to be "with him." In fact, this personal appointment to be in constant association with him was as much a part of their ordination commission as the authority to evangelize. Indeed, it was for the moment even more important, for it was the necessary preparation for the other.

Closer as Training Ends

The determination with which Jesus sought to fulfill this commission is evident as one reads through the subsequent Gospel accounts. Contrary to what one might expect, as the ministry of Christ lengthened into the second and third years he gave increasingly more time to the chosen disciples, not less.[1]

Frequently he would take them with him on a retreat to some mountainous area of the country where he was relatively unknown, seeking to avoid publicity as far as possible. They took trips together to Tyre and Sidon to the northwest (Mark 7:24; Matt. 15:21); to the "borders of Decapolis" (Mark 7:31; cf., Matt. 15:29) and "the parts of Dalmanutha" to the southeast of Galilee (Mark 8:10; cf., Matt. 15:39); and to the "villages of Caesarea Philippi" to the northeast (Mark 8:27; cf., Matt. 16:13). These journeys were made partly because of the opposition of the Pharisees and the hostility of Herod, but primarily because Jesus felt the need to get alone with his disciples. Later he spent several months with his disciples in Perea, east of the Jordan (Luke 13:22–19:28; John 10:40–11:54; Matt. 19:1–20:34; Mark 10:1–52). As opposition mounted there, Jesus "walked no more openly among the Jews, but departed thence into the country near to the wilderness, into a city called Ephraim; and there he tarried with his disciples" (John 11:54). When at last the time came for him to go to Jerusalem, he significantly "took the twelve disciples apart" from the rest as he made his way slowly to the city (Matt. 20:17; cf., Mark 10:32).

In view of this, it is not surprising that during passion week Jesus scarcely ever let his disciples out of his sight. Even when he prayed alone in Gethsemane, his disciples were only a stone's throw away (Luke 22:41). Is not this the way it is with every family as the hour of departing draws near? Every minute is cherished because of the growing realization that such close association in the flesh soon will be no more. Words uttered under these circumstances are always more precious. Indeed, it was not until time began to close in that the disciples of Christ were prepared to grasp many of the deeper meanings of his presence with them (John 16:4). Doubtless this explains why the writers of the Gospels were constrained to devote so much of their attention to these last days. Fully half of all that is recorded about Jesus happened in the last months of his life, and most of this in the last week.

The course followed by Jesus through life was supremely portrayed in the days following his resurrection. Interestingly enough, every one of the ten postresurrection appearances of Christ was to his followers, particularly the chosen apostles.[2] So far as the Bible shows, not one unbelieving person was permitted to see the glorified Lord. Yet it is not so strange. There was no need to excite the multitudes with his spectacular revelation. What could they have done? But the disciples who had fled in despair following the crucifixion needed to be revived in their faith and confirmed in their mission to the world. His whole ministry evolved around them.

And so it was. The time which Jesus invested in these few disciples was so much more by comparison to that given to others that it can only be regarded as a deliberate strategy. He actually spent more time with his disciples than with everybody else in the world put together. He ate with them, slept with them, and talked with them for the most part of his entire active ministry. They walked together along the lonely roads; they visited together in the crowded cities; they sailed and fished together on the Sea of Galilee; they prayed together in the deserts and in the mountains; and they worshiped together in the synagogues and in the Temple.

Still Ministering to the Masses

One must not overlook that even while Jesus was ministering to others, the disciples were always there with him. Whether he addressed the multitudes that pressed on him, conversed with the scribes and Pharisees which sought to ensnare him, or spoke to some lonely beggar along the road, the disciples were close at hand to observe and to listen. In this manner, Jesus' time was paying double dividends. Without neglecting his regular ministry to those in need, he maintained a constant ministry to his disciples by having them with him. They were thus getting the benefit of everything he said and did to others plus their own personal explanation and counsel.

It Takes Time

Such close and constant association, of course, meant that Jesus had virtually no time to call his own. Like little children clamoring for the attention of their father, the disciples were always under foot of the Master. Even the time he took to go apart to keep his personal devotions was subject to interruption at the disciples' need (Mark 6:46–48; cf., Luke 11:1). But Jesus would have it no other way. He wanted to be with them. They were his spiritual children (Mark 10:24; John 13:33; 21:5), and the only way that a father can properly raise a family is to be with it.

The Foundation of Follow-up

Nothing is more obvious yet more neglected than the application of this principle. By its very nature, it does not call attention to itself, and one is prone to overlook the commonplace. Yet Jesus would not let his disciples miss it. During the last days of his journey, the Master especially felt it necessary to crystallize their thinking about what he had been doing. For example, once turning to these who had followed him for three years, Jesus said: "Ye [shall] bear witness because ye have been with me from the beginning" (John 15:27). Without any fanfare and unnoticed by the world, Jesus was saying that he had been training men to be his witnesses after he had gone, and his method of doing it was simply by being "with them." Indeed, as he said on another occasion, it was because they had "continued with" him in his temptations that they were appointed to be leaders in his eternal kingdom where they would each eat and drink at his table, and sit on thrones judging the twelve tribes of Israel (Luke 22:28–30).

It would be wrong to assume, however, that this principle of personal follow-up was confined only to the apostolic band. Jesus concentrated on these few chosen men, but also manifested concern for others who followed him. For example, he went home with Zacchaeus after his conversion on the streets of Jericho (Luke 19:7), and he spent some time with him before leaving the city. After the conversion of the woman at the well in Samaria, Jesus tarried two extra days in Sychar to instruct the people of that community who "believed on him because of the word of the woman who testified," and because of that personal association with them "many more believed," not because of the woman's witness, but because they heard for themselves the Master (John 4:39–42). Often one who received some help from the Master would be permitted to join the procession following Jesus, as for example, Bartimaeus (Mark 10:52; Matt. 20:34; Luke 18:43). In such a way many attached themselves to the apostolic company, as is evidenced by the seventy with him in the later Judean ministry (Luke 10:1, 17). All of these believers received some personal attention, but it could not be compared to that given to the Twelve.

Mention should be made, too, of that small group of faithful women who ministered to him out of their substance, like Mary and Martha (Luke 10:38–42), Mary Magdalene, Joanna, Susanna, "and many others" (Luke 8:1–3). Some of these women were with him to the end. He certainly did not refuse their gracious kindness, and often took the occasion to help them in their faith. Jesus welcomed their assistance but did not try to incorporate these women into the select company of his chosen disciples.

Jesus did not have the time to personally give all these people, men or women, constant attention. He did all that he could, and this doubtless served to impress on his disciples the need for immediate personal care of new converts, but he had to devote himself primarily to the task of developing some leaders who in turn could give this kind of personal attention to others.

The Church as a Continuing Fellowship

Really the whole problem of giving personal care to every believer is only resolved in a thorough understanding of the nature and mission of the church. It is well here to observe that the emergence of the church principle around Jesus, whereby one believer was brought into fellowship with all others, was the practice in a larger dimension of the same thing that he was doing with the Twelve.[3] Actually it was the church that was the means of following up all those who followed him. That is, the group of believers became the body of Christ, and as such ministered to each other individually and collectively.

Every member of the community of faith had a part to fulfill in this ministry. But this they could only do as they themselves were trained and inspired. As long as Jesus was with them in the flesh, he was the Leader, but thereafter, it was necessary for those in the church to assume this leadership. Again this meant that Jesus had to train them to do it, which involved his own constant personal association with a few chosen men.

Our Problem

When will the church learn this lesson? Preaching to the masses, although necessary, will never suffice in the work of preparing leaders for evangelism. Nor can occasional prayer meetings and training classes for Christian workers do this job. Building men and women is not that easy. It requires constant personal attention, much like a father gives to his children. This is something that no organization or class can ever do. Children are not raised by proxy. The example of Jesus would teach us that it can be done only by persons staying close to those whom they seek to lead.

The church obviously has failed at this point, and failed tragically. There is a lot of talk in the church about evangelism and Christian nurture, but little concern for personal association when it becomes evident that such work involves the sacrifice of personal indulgence. Of course, most churches insist on bringing new members through some kind of a confirmation class which usually meets an hour a week for a month or so. But the rest of the time the young convert has no contact with a definite Christian training program, except as he or she may attend the worship services of the church and the Sunday school. Unless new Christians, if indeed they are saved, have parents or friends who will fill the gap in a real way, they are left entirely on their own to find the solutions to innumerable practical problems confronting their lives, any one of which could mean disaster to their new faith.

With such haphazard follow-up of believers, it is no wonder that about half of those who make professions and join the church eventually fall away or lose the glow of a Christian experience, and fewer still grow in sufficient knowledge and grace to be of any real service to the Kingdom. If Sunday services and membership training classes are all that a church has to develop young converts into mature disciples, then they are defeating their own purpose by contributing to a false security, and if the new convert follows the same lazy example, it may ultimately do more harm than good. There is simply no substitute for getting with people, and it is ridiculous to imagine that anything less, short of a miracle, can develop strong Christian leadership. After all, if Jesus, the Son of God, found it necessary to stay almost constantly with his few disciples for three years, and even one of them was lost, how can a church expect to do this job on an assembly line basis a few days out of the year?

The Principle Applied Today

Clearly the policy of Jesus at this point teaches us that whatever method of follow-up the church adopts, it must have as its basis a personal guardian concern for those entrusted to their care. To do otherwise is essentially to abandon new believers to the devil.

This means that some system must be found whereby every convert is given a Christian friend to follow until such time as he or she can lead another. The counselor should stay with the new believer as much as possible, studying the Bible and praying with him or her, all the while answering questions, clarifying the truth, and seeking together to help others. If a church does not have such committed counselors willing to do this service, then it should be training some. And the only way they can be trained is by giving them a leader to follow.

This answers the question of how it is to be done, but it is necessary now to understand that this method can accomplish its purpose only when the followers practice what they learn. Hence, another basic principle in the Master's strategy must be understood.

Take my yoke upon you
Matthew 11:29

3

Consecration

He Required Obedience

Jesus expected the men he was with to obey him. They were not required to be smart, but they had to be loyal. This became the distinguishing mark by which they were known. They were called his "disciples" meaning that they were "learners" or "pupils" of the Master. It was not until much later that they started to be called "Christian" (Acts 11:26), although it was inevitable, for in time obedient followers invariably take on the character of their leader.

The simplicity of this approach is marvelous if not astounding. None of the disciples was asked at first to make a statement of faith or accept a well-defined creed, although they doubtless recognized Jesus to be the Messiah (John 1:41, 45, 49; Luke 5:8). For the moment all they were asked to do was to follow Jesus. Of course, clearly implied in their initial invitation was a call to faith in the person of Christ and obedience to his Word. If this was not comprehended in the beginning, it would be perceived as they continued in the way with the Master. No one will follow a person in whom he or she has no trust, nor sincerely take the step of faith unless he or she is willing to obey what the leader says.

The Way of the Cross

Following Jesus seemed easy enough at first, but that was because they had not followed him very far. It soon became apparent that being a disciple of Christ involved far more than a joyful acceptance of the Messianic promise: it meant the surrender of one's whole life to the Master in absolute submission to his sovereignty. There could be no compromise. "No servant can serve two masters," Jesus said, "for either he will hate the one, and love the other; or else he will hold to one, and despise the other. Ye cannot serve God and mammon" (Luke 16:13). There had to be a complete forsaking of sin. The old thought patterns, habits, and pleasures of the world had to be conformed to the new disciplines of the kingdom of God (Matt. 5:1–7:29; Luke 6:20–49). Perfection of love was now the only standard of conduct (Matt. 5:48), and this love was to manifest itself in obedience to Christ (John 14:21, 23) expressed in devotion to those whom he died to save (Matt. 25:31–36). There was a cross in it—the willing denial of self for others (Mark 8:34–38; 10:32–45; Matt. 16:24–26; 20:17–28; Luke 9:23–25; John 12:25, 26; 13:1–20).

This was strong teaching. Not many people could take it. They liked to be numbered among his followers when he filled their stomachs with bread and fish, but when Jesus started talking about the true spiritual quality of the Kingdom and the sacrifice necessary in achieving it (John 6:25–59), many of his disciples "went back, and walked no more with him" (John 6:66). As they put it, "This is a hard saying: who can hear it?" (John 6:60). The surprising thing is that Jesus did not go running after them to try to get them to stay on his membership roll. He was training leaders for the Kingdom, and if they were going to be fit vessels of service, they were going to have to pay the price.

Count the Cost

Those who would not go all the way thus in time fell by the wayside. They separated themselves from the chosen company by reason of their own selfishness. Judas, exposed as a devil (John 6:70), held on until the end, but at last his greed caught up with him (Mark 14:10, 11, 43, 44; Matt. 26:14–16, 47–50; Luke 22:3–6, 47–49; John 18:2–9). One simply could not follow Jesus through the course of his life without turning loose of the world, and those who made a pretense of it brought only anguish and tragedy to their souls (Matt. 27:3–10; Acts 1:18, 19).

Perhaps this is why Jesus spoke so severely to the scribe who came and said, "Master, I will follow thee whithersoever thou goest." Jesus frankly told this apparent volunteer for service that it would not be easy. "The foxes have holes and the birds of the air have nests; but the Son of man hath not where to lay his head" (Matt. 8:19, 20; Luke 9:57, 58). Another disciple wanted to be excused from his immediate obligation of obedience so that he might go and care for his aged father, but Jesus would allow no delay. "Follow me," he said, "and leave the dead to bury the dead. Go thou and publish abroad the kingdom of God" (Matt. 8:21, 22; Luke 9:59, 60). Another man indicated that he would follow Jesus, but on his own terms. He wanted to first bid farewell to his family, perhaps anticipating a merry good time doing it. But Jesus put it to him straight. "No man, having put his hand to the plough, and looking back is fit for the kingdom of God" (Luke 9:62). Jesus did not have the time nor the desire to scatter himself on those who wanted to make their own terms of discipleship.

Hence it was that a would-be disciple was made to count the cost. "For which of you, desiring to build a tower, doth not first sit down and count the cost, whether he have wherewith to complete it?" (Luke 14:28). Not to do so was tantamount to inviting ridicule later from the world. The same would be true of a king in war who did not consider the cost of victory before hostilities began. To sum it up bluntly, Jesus said: "Therefore whosoever he be of you that renounceth not all that he hath, he cannot be my disciple" (Luke 14:33; cf., Mark 10:21; Matt. 19:21; Luke 18:22).

Few Would Pay the Price

Actually when the opportunists left him at Capernaum because he would not satisfy their popular expectations, Jesus had only a handful of followers left. Turning to the Twelve, he said, "Would ye also go away?" (John 6:67). This was a crucial question. If these few men quit following him, what would remain of his ministry? But Simon Peter answered, "Lord, to whom shall we go? thou hast the words of eternal life. And we have believed and know that thou art the Holy One of God" (John 6:68, 69). Indeed these words of the apostle must have been reassuring to the Master, for thereafter Jesus began to talk with his disciples more about his suffering and death, and with greater frankness.[1]

To Obey Is to Learn

This does not mean, however, that the disciples quickly understood everything the Lord said. Far from it. Their ability to grasp the deeper truths of the Lord's vicarious ministry was encumbered with all the limitations of human frailty. When Jesus told the disciples after the great affirmation at Caesarea Philippi that he would be put to death by the religious leaders in Jerusalem, Peter actually rebuked him, saying, "Be it far from thee, Lord: This shall never be unto thee" (Matt. 16:22; cf., Mark 8:32). Whereupon Jesus had to tell the big fisherman that Satan deceived him at this point, "For thou mindest not the things of God, but of men" (Matt. 16:23; Mark 8:33). Nor did this end it. Again and again Jesus felt constrained to speak about his death, and its meaning to them, but they failed to comprehend it until the day he was betrayed into the hands of his enemies.

Not comprehending clearly the message of the cross, of course, they faltered at first in understanding their own place in the Kingdom. It was hard for them to accept the teaching of lowly servitude for the sake of others (Luke 22:24–30; John 13:1–20). They bickered among themselves who would be greatest in the Kingdom (Mark 9:33–37; Matt. 18:1–5; Luke 9:46–48). James and John wanted to have the prominent places (Mark 10:35–37; Matt. 20:20), and the other ten, displaying an envious spirit, were indignant about it (Mark 10:41; Matt. 20:24). They were unnecessarily harsh in their judgment on others who did not agree with them (Luke 9:51–54). They were moved "with indignation" at parents who wanted Jesus to bless their children (Mark 10:13). Obviously, the practical outworking of what it meant to follow Christ was not fully experienced.

Yet Jesus patiently endured these human failings of his chosen disciples because in spite of all their shortcomings they were willing to follow him. There was a brief interval of time after their initial call when they went back to their old fishing business (Mark 1:16; Matt. 4:18; Luke 5:2–5; cf., John 1:35–42), but their return does not seem to have been precipitated by any act of disobedience on their part. They just had not come to realize his purpose for their lives in leadership, or perhaps it had not yet been told them. Nonetheless, from the time that he appeared at their business and asked them to follow him to become fishers of men, "they left all, and followed him" (Luke 5:11; cf., Matt. 4:22, Mark 1:20). Later on, though they had much to learn, they could say that their dedication to Christ was still holding true (Mark 10:28; Matt. 19:27; Luke 18:28). With such men Jesus was willing to put up with a lot of those things which issued from their spiritual immaturity. He knew that they could master these defects as they grew in grace and knowledge. Their capacity to receive revelation would grow provided they continued to practice what truth they did understand.

Obedience to Christ thus was the very means by which those in his company learned more truth. He did not ask the disciples to follow what they did not know to be true, but no one could follow him without learning what was true (John 7:17). Hence, Jesus did not urge his disciples to commit their lives to a doctrine, but to a person who was the doctrine, and only as they continued in his Word could they know the truth (John 8:31, 32).

The Proof of Love

Supreme obedience was interpreted to be the expression of love. This lesson was underscored most emphatically on the eve of his death. As the disciples gathered around him in the upper room following the paschal meal, Jesus said: "If ye love me, ye will keep my commandments. . . . He that hath my commandments, and keepeth them, he it is that loveth me; and he shall be loved of my Father, and I will love him, and will manifest myself unto him. . . . If a man love me, he will keep my word; and my Father will love him, and we will come unto him and make our abode with him. He that loveth me not keepeth not my words; and the word which ye hear is not mine, but the Father's which sent me. . . . If ye keep my commandments, ye shall abide in my love. . . . This is my commandment, That ye love one another, as I have loved

you. Ye are my friends if ye do whatsoever I have told you"
(John 14:15, 21, 23, 24; 15:10, 12).

Demonstrated by Jesus

Absolute obedience to the will of God, of course, was the
controlling principle of the Master's own life. In his human
nature he continually gave consent to the will of his Father
which made it possible for God to use his life fully according
to its intended purpose. Repeatedly he sounded it out: "My
meat is to do the will of him that sent me, and to accomplish
his work" (John 4:34); "I seek not my own will, but the will
of him that sent me" (John 5:30; cf., 6:38); "I have kept my
Father's commandments and abide in his love" (John 15:10;
cf., 17:4). It could be summed up in his cry of Gethsemane,
"Not my will, but thine be done" (Luke 22:42; cf., Mark
14:36; Matt. 26:39, 42, 44).

The cross was but the crowning climax of Jesus' commitment to do the will of God. It forever showed that obedience could not be compromised—it was always a commitment unto death.

The worldly-minded religious leaders stated the truth
when they said in derision: "He saved others; himself he cannot save" (Mark 15:31; Matt. 27:42; Luke 23:35). Of course,
he could not save himself. He had not come to save himself.
He came to save the world. He came "not to be ministered
unto, but to minister, and to give his life a ransom for many"
(Mark 10:45; Matt. 20:28). He came "to seek and to save
that which was lost" (Luke 19:10). He came to offer himself a sacrifice unto God for the sins of all people. He came
to die. There was no other way that the inviolable law of God
could be satisfied.

This cross, having already been accepted in advance (Rev.
13:8; cf., Acts 2:32), made each step that Christ took on the

earth a conscious acceptance of God's eternal purpose for his life. When Jesus therefore spoke about obedience, it was something which the disciples could see incarnated in human form. As Jesus put it, "Ye should do as I have done unto you. Verily, verily, I say unto you, a servant is not greater than his lord; neither he that is sent greater than he that sent him. If ye know these things, blessed are ye if ye do them" (John 13:15, 16). No one could miss this lesson. Just as Jesus found his blessedness in doing his Father's will, even so his followers would find theirs. This is the sole duty of a servant. It was true of Christ, and nothing less can ever be accepted as worthy of his disciple (Luke 17:6–10; cf., 8:21; Mark 3:35; Matt. 12:50).

The Principle in Focus

From the standpoint of strategy, however, it was the only way that Jesus could mold their lives by his word. There could be no development of character or purpose in the disciples without it. A father must teach his children to obey him if he expects his children to be like him.

It must be remembered, too, that Jesus was making men to lead his church to conquest, and no one can ever be a leader until first he has learned to follow a leader. So he brought up his future commanders from the ranks, drilling in them along the way the necessity for discipline and respect for authority. There could be no insubordination in his command. No one knew better than Jesus that the satanic forces of darkness against them were well organized and equipped to make ineffectual any half-hearted effort of evangelism. They could not possibly outwit the devilish powers of this world unless they gave strict adherence to him who alone knew the strategy of victory. This required absolute obedience to the Master's will, even as it meant complete abandonment of their own.

The Principle Applied Today

We must learn this lesson again today. There can be no dillydallying around with the commands of Christ. We are engaged in warfare, the issues of which are life and death, and every day that we are indifferent to our responsibilities is a day lost to the cause of Christ. If we have learned even the most elemental truth of discipleship, we must know that we are called to be servants of our Lord and to obey his Word. It is not our duty to reason why he speaks as he does, but only to carry out his orders. Unless there is this dedication to all that we know he wants us to do now, however immature our understanding may be, it is doubtful if we will ever progress further in his life and mission. There is no place in the Kingdom for a slacker, for such an attitude not only precludes any growth in grace and knowledge, but also destroys any usefulness on the world battlefield of evangelism.

One must ask, why are so many professed Christians today stunted in their growth and ineffectual in their witness? Or to put the question in its larger context, why is the contemporary church so frustrated in its witness to the world? Is it not because among the clergy and laity alike there is a general indifference to the commands of God, or at least, a kind of contented complacency with mediocrity? Where is the obedience of the cross? Indeed, it would appear that the teachings of Christ regarding self-denial and dedication have been replaced by a sort of respectable "do-as-you-please" philosophy of expediency.

The great tragedy is that little is being done to correct the situation, even by those who realize what is happening. Certainly the need of the hour is not for despair, but for action.

It is high time that the requirements for membership in the church be interpreted and enforced in terms of true Christian discipleship. But this action alone will not be enough. Followers must have leaders, and this means that before much can be done with the church membership something will have to be done with the church officials. If this task seems to be too great, then we will have to start like Jesus did by getting with a few chosen ones and instilling into them the meaning of obedience.

It is when this principle is accepted in practice that we can develop fully according to the next step in the Master's strategy of conquest.

4
Impartation

He Gave Himself Away

Jesus wanted his followers to obey him. But in recognizing this truth, he realized that his disciples would discover the deeper experience of his Spirit. And in receiving his Spirit they would know the love of God for a lost world. That is why his demands were accepted without argument. The disciples understood that they were not just keeping a law, but were responding to One who loved them, and was willing to give himself for them.

His was a life of giving—giving away what the Father had given him (John 15:15; 17:4, 8, 14). He gave them his peace by which he was sustained in tribulation (John 16:33; cf., Matt. 11:28). He gave them his joy in which he labored amid the sufferings and sorrows about him (John 15:11; 17:13). He gave them the keys to his Kingdom against which the powers of hell could never prevail (Matt. 16:19; cf., Luke 12:32). Indeed, he gave them his own glory which was his before the worlds were made, that they all might be one even as he was one in the Father (John 17:22, 24). He gave all he had—nothing was withheld, not even his own life.

Love is like that. It is always giving itself away. When it is self-contained, it is not love. In this sense, Jesus brought clearly into focus before his followers just what was meant when "God so loved the world" (John 3:16). It meant that God gave all he had to those he loved, even his "only begotten Son." And for the Son, in incarnating that love, it meant renouncing his own right of living and giving his life for the world. Only in this light—when the Son is put in place of the world—can one even begin to understand the cross. Yet in this realization, the cross of Christ is inevitable, for the infinite love of God can express itself only in an infinite way. Just as man by his sin had to die, so God by his love had to send his Son to die in our place. "Greater love hath no man than this, that a man lay down his life for his friends" (John 15:13).

The Compulsion of Evangelism

That is why he lost no opportunity to impress on his followers the deep compulsion of his own soul aflame with the love of God for a lost world. Everything he did and said was motivated by this consuming passion. His life was simply the revelation in time of God's eternal purpose to save for himself a people. Supremely this is what the disciples needed to learn, not in theory, but in practice.

And they saw it practiced before them in many ways every day. Though the demonstrations were often painfully hard to accept, as when he washed their feet (John 13:1–20), they could not miss what he meant. They saw how their Master denied himself many of the comforts and pleasures of the world and became a servant among them. They saw how the things which they cherished—physical satisfaction, popular acclaim, prestige—he refused; while the things which they sought to escape—poverty, humiliation, sorrow, and even death—he accepted willingly for their sake. As they watched him minister to the sick, comfort the sorrowing, and preach the gospel to the poor, it was clear that the Master considered no service too small nor sacrifice too great when it was rendered for the glory of God. They may not have always understood it, and certainly could not explain it, but they could never mistake it.

His Sanctification

The constant renewing of his consecration of himself to God through loving service to others constituted Jesus' sanctification. This was brought out clearly in his highpriestly prayer when he said: "As thou didst send me into the world, even so sent I them into the world. And for their sakes I sanctify myself, that they themselves also may be sanctified in truth" (John 17:18, 19). Note that this setting apart of himself unto God, which is indicated in the word *sanctify*, was not necessary in Jesus' case to effect cleansing, since he was always pure. Nor was it necessary to receive power for service, since Jesus already had all the power he could use. Rather his sanctification, as the context reveals, was in the area of commitment to the task for which he had been "sent into the world,"[1] and in dedication to that purpose of evangelism, he continually gave his life "for their sakes."

His sanctification then was not for the purpose of benefiting himself, but it was for his disciples, that they might "be sanctified in truth."[2] That is to say, in giving himself to God, Jesus gave himself to those about him so that they might come to know through his life a similar commitment to the mission for which he had come into the world. His whole evangelistic plan hinged on this dedication, and in turn, the faithfulness with which his disciples gave themselves in love to the world about them.

Credentials of the Ministry

This was to be the measure by which they were to regard their own service in his name. They were to give as freely as they had received (Matt. 10:8). They were to love one another as he loved them (John 13:34, 35). By this token they were to be his disciples (John 15:9, 10). Herein was contained all his commandments (John 15:12, 17; cf., Matt. 22:37–40; Mark 12:30, 31; Luke 10:27). Love—Calvary love—was the standard. Just as they had seen for three years, the disciples were to give themselves in selfless devotion to those whom the Father loved and for whom their Master died (John 17:23).

Such a demonstration of love through them was to be the way that the world would know that the Gospel was true. How else would the multitudes ever be convinced? Love is the only way to win the free response of men, and this is possible only by the presence of Christ within the heart. Thus Jesus prayed: "O righteous Father, the world knew thee not, but I knew thee; and these knew that thou didst send me; and I made known unto them thy name, and will make it known; that the love wherewith thou lovedst me may be in them, and I in them" (John 17:25, 26).

The Work of the Holy Spirit

Let no one imagine, however, that this kind of an experience with Christ could be engendered by human ingenuity. Jesus made it abundantly clear that his life was mediated only through the Holy Spirit. "It is the Spirit that quickeneth; the flesh profiteth nothing" (John 6:63). That is why even to begin to live in Christ one had to be born again (John 3:3–9). The corrupted human nature must be regenerated by the Spirit of God before it could be conformed to its true created purpose in the divine image. Likewise, it is the Spirit who sustains and nourishes the transformed life of a disciple in knowledge and grace (John 4:14; 7:38, 39). By the same Spirit one is made clean through the Word and set apart unto God for holy service (John 15:3; 17:17; cf., Eph. 5:26). From beginning to end, experiencing the living Christ in any personal way is the work of the Holy Spirit.

It is only the Spirit of God who enables one to carry on the redemptive mission of evangelism. Jesus underscored this truth early in relation to his own work by declaring that what he did was in cooperation with "the Spirit of the Lord." It was by his virtue that he preached the gospel to the poor, healed the brokenhearted, proclaimed deliverance to the captive, opened the eyes of the blind, cast out demons, and set at liberty those that were oppressed (Luke 4:18; Matt. 12: 28). Jesus was God in revelation; but the Spirit was God in operation. He was the Agent of God actually effecting through men the eternal plan of salvation. Thus Jesus explained to his disciples that the Spirit would prepare the way for their ministry. He would give them utterance to speak (Matt. 10:19, 20; Mark 13:11; Luke 12:12). He would convict the world "in respect of sin, and of righteousness, and of judgment" (John 16:8). He would give illumination of truth that men might know the Lord (Matt. 22:43; cf., Mark 12:36; John 16:14). By his power the disciples were promised the very ability to do the works of their Lord (John 14:12).[3] In this light, evangelism was not interpreted as a human undertaking, but as a divine project which had been going on from the beginning and would continue until God's purpose was fulfilled. It was altogether the Spirit's work. All the disciples were asked to do was to let the Spirit have complete charge of their lives.

Another Comforter

From the standpoint of their own satisfaction, however, the disciples needed to learn in a more meaningful way the relationship of the Spirit to the person of their Lord. Jesus, of course, recognized this need, and therefore he spoke more specifically about it as the days of his flesh came to a close. Up to this point he had always been with them. He had been their Comforter, their Teacher, their Guide. In fellowship with him the disciples had known courage and strength; with him they felt that everything was possible; but their trouble was that Jesus was going back to heaven. Under these circumstances Jesus needed to explain to them how they would get along after he had gone.

It was at this time that Jesus told them about the Spirit as "Another Comforter,"[4] an Advocate, one who would stand by their side, a person who would take exactly the same place with them in the unseen realm of reality that Jesus had filled in the visible experience of the flesh (John 14:16). Just as he had ministered to them for three years, now the Spirit would guide them into all truth (John 16:13). He would show them things to come (John 16:13). He would teach them what they needed to know (John 14:26). He would help them pray (John 14:12, 13; 16:23, 24). In short, he would glorify the Son by taking the things of Christ and making them real to his followers (John 16:14, 15). The world could not receive this truth, for it did not know Jesus; but the disciples knew him, for he was with them, and in the Spirit, he would continue to be with them forever (John 14:17).

This was no theory, no creed, no makeshift arrangement that Jesus was talking about. It was the promise of a real compensation for the loss which the disciples were to sustain. "Another Comforter" just like Jesus was to fill them with the very presence of the Master. Indeed, the privileges which the disciples were to enjoy in this deeper relationship to the Spirit were greater than they had known as Jesus walked with them along the roads of Galilee. After all, in his flesh, Jesus was confined to one body and one place, but in the Spirit these limitations were all removed. Now he could be with them always, and literally be enabled never to leave them nor forsake them (Matt. 28:20; cf., John 14:16). Looking at it from this perspective, it was better for Jesus, having finished his work, to return to the Father and send the blessed Comforter to come and take his place (John 16:7).

The Secret of the Victorious Life

It is easy to see then why Jesus expected his disciples to tarry until this promise became a reality to them (Luke 24:49; Acts 1:4, 5, 8; 2:33). How else could they ever fulfill the commission of their Lord with joy and inward peace? They needed an experience of Christ so real that their lives would be filled with his presence. Evangelism had to become a burning compulsion within them purifying their desires and guiding their thoughts. Nothing less than a personal baptism of the Holy Spirit would suffice. The superhuman work to which they were called demanded supernatural help—an enduement of power from on high. This meant that the disciples through confession of their deep-seated pride and enmity in utter surrender of themselves to Christ had to come by faith into a new and refining experience of the Spirit's infilling.[5]

The fact that these men were of the common lot of mankind was no hindrance at all. It only serves to remind us of the mighty power of the Spirit of God accomplishing his purpose in disciples fully yielded to his control. After all, the power is in the Spirit of Christ. It is not who we are, but who he is that makes the difference.

A Truth Hidden from Unbelievers

However, it is well to mention again that only those who followed Jesus all the way came to know the glory of this experience. Those who followed at a distance, like the multitudes, as well as those who stubbornly refused to walk in the light of his Word, like the Pharisees, did not even hear about the work of the blessed Comforter. As noted before, Jesus would not cast his pearls before those who did not want them.[6]

This characterized his teaching throughout life. Jesus purposely reserved for his few chosen disciples, and particularly the Twelve, his most revealing things (Luke 10:22; Matt. 11:27; cf., 16:17). Indeed, their eyes and ears were blessed. Many prophets and kings had desired to see the things which they saw, and to hear the things which they heard, yet could not (Matt. 13:16, 17; Luke 10:23, 24; cf., Matt. 13:10, 11; Mark 4:10, 11; Luke 8:9, 10). Such a policy may seem strange until we remember that Jesus was deliberately investing all he had in these few men so that they could be properly prepared to do his work.

The Principle Issue Today

The whole thing revolves around the person of the Master. Basically his way was his life. And so it must be with his followers. We must have his life in us by the Spirit if we are to do his work and practice his teaching. Any evangelistic work without this is as lifeless as it is meaningless. Only as the Spirit of Christ in us exalts the Son are people drawn unto the Father.

Of course, we cannot give something away which we do not possess ourselves. The very ability to give away our life in Christ is the proof of its possession. Nor can we withhold that which we possess in the Spirit of Christ, and still keep it. The Spirit of God always insists on making Christ known. Here is the great paradox of life—we must die to ourselves to live in Christ, and in that renunciation of ourselves, we must give ourselves away in service and devotion to our Lord. This was Jesus' method of evangelism, seen at first only by his few followers, but through them it was to become the power of God in overcoming the world.

But we cannot stop there. It is also necessary for one to see in us a clear demonstration of the way to live his life. Thus, we must understand another obvious aspect of Jesus' strategy with his disciples.

I have given you an example
John 13:15

5

Demonstration

He Showed Them How to Live

Jesus saw to it that his disciples learned his way of living with God and man. He recognized that it was not enough just to get people into his spiritual communion. His disciples needed to know how his experience was to be maintained and shared if it was to be perpetuated in evangelism. Of course, in a technical sense, life precedes action, but in a thoroughly practical point of view, we live by what we do. We must breathe, eat, exercise, and carry on work normally if we are to grow. Where these functions of the body are neglected, life will cease to be. That is why the effort of Jesus to get across to his followers the secrets of his spiritual influence needs to be considered as a deliberate course of his master strategy. He knew what was important.

The Practice of Prayer

Take, for example, his prayer life. Surely it was no accident that Jesus often let his disciples see him conversing with the

Father.[1] They could see the strength which it gave to his life, and though they could not understand fully what it was all about, they must have realized that this was part of his secret of life. Note that Jesus did not force the lesson on them, but rather he just kept praying until at last the disciples got so hungry that they asked him to teach them what he was doing.

Seizing his opportunity when it did come, Jesus proceeded to give them a lesson which their hearts were prepared to receive. He explained to them some of the more basic principles of prayer, and then before he finished, he illustrated what he meant by repeating before them a model prayer (Luke 11:1–4; Matt. 6:9–13). One might possibly think that such a practice was below the capabilities of these disciples— the idea of having to put words in their mouths to get them to pray—but Jesus would not take such an important matter as this for granted. Indeed, such elementary methods of teaching are often necessary to get people started in this discipline. But whatever it took, Jesus was determined to get this lesson across.

Thereafter he emphasized the life of prayer again and again when talking with his disciples, continually enlarging on its meaning and application as they were able to comprehend deeper realities of his Spirit. It was an indispensable part of their training, which in turn they would have to transmit to others. One thing is certain. Unless they grasped the meaning of prayer, and learned how to practice it with consistency, not much would ever come from their lives.

Using Scripture

Another aspect of Jesus' life which was vividly portrayed to the disciples was the importance and use of the Holy Scriptures.[2] This was evident both in maintaining his own personal devotion and in winning others to the Way. Often he would take special pains to impress on his followers the meaning of some passage in the Bible, and he never ceased to use the Scriptures in his conversation with them. Altogether there are at least sixty-six references to the Old Testament in his dialogues with the disciples in the four Gospels, to say nothing of the more than ninety allusions to it in his speaking with others.[3]

All this served to show the disciples how they too should know and use the Scriptures in their own life. The principles of Bible exhortation were practiced before them so repeatedly that they could not help but catch on to at least some of the rules for basic Scriptural interpretation and application. Moreover, the ability of Jesus to recall so freely Old Testament passages must have impressed the disciples with the necessity of learning the Scriptures by heart, and letting them become the authority for their pronouncements.

In everything it was made abundantly clear that the word written in the Scriptures and the word spoken by Christ were not in contradiction, but rather complemented each other. That which Jesus taught was also to be cherished by his disciples. Hence, the Scriptures, coupled with his own utterance, became for them the objective basis of their faith in Christ. Furthermore, it was made clear to them that if they were to continue in his fellowship by the Spirit after he was gone from them in the flesh, they would have to abide in his Word (John 15:7).

Supremely Soul Winning

Through this manner of personal demonstration, every aspect of Jesus' personal discipline of life was bequeathed to his disciples,[4] but what perhaps was most important in view of his ultimate purpose was that all the while he was teaching them how to win souls.

Practically everything that Jesus said and did had some relevance to their work of evangelism, either by explaining a spiritual truth or revealing to them how they should deal with people. He did not have to work up teaching situations, but merely took advantage of those about him, and thus his teaching seemed perfectly realistic. In fact, for the most part, the disciples were absorbing it without even knowing that they were being trained to win people under like conditions for God.

Teaching Naturally

This point, already alluded to several times, cannot be emphasized too much. Jesus was so much the Master in his teaching that he did not let his method obscure his lesson. He let his truth call attention to itself, and not the presentation.[5] His method in this respect was to conceal the fact that he even had a method. He was his method.

This may be hard to imagine in this day of professional techniques and sure-fire gimmicks. In some quarters, it would almost appear we would be unable to proceed without a well-illustrated handbook or multicolored flip chart showing us what to do. The least we might expect is a seminar in soul winning. Yet, strange as it may seem, the disciples never had any of these things now considered so essential for the work.

All the disciples had to teach them was a teacher who practiced with them what he expected them to learn. Evangelism was lived before them in spirit and in technique. Watching him, they learned what it was all about. He led them to recognize the need inherent in all classes of people, and the best methods of approaching them. They observed how he drew people to himself; how he won their confidence and inspired their faith; how he opened to them the way of salvation and called them to a decision. In all types of situations and among all kinds of people, rich and poor, healthy and sick, friend and foe alike, the disciples watched the master soulwinner at work. It wasn't outlined on the blackboard of a stuffy classroom nor written up in a "do it yourself" manual. His method was so real and practical that it just came naturally.

Classes Always in Session

This was as true in his approach to the masses as his way of dealing with individuals. The disciples were always there to observe his word and deed. If the particular approach was not clear, all they had to do was to ask the Master to explain it to them. For example, after Jesus told the story of the sower to "a very great multitude" (Mark 4:1f.; cf., Matt. 13:1–9; Luke 8:4–8), his disciples "asked him what this parable might be" (Luke 8:9; cf., Mark 4:10; Matt. 13:10). Whereupon Jesus proceeded to explain to them in detail the meaning of the analogies used in the illustration. In fact, judging from the printed text, he spent three times the amount of time explaining this story to the disciples than he did in giving the initial lesson to the crowd (Matt. 13:10–23; Mark 4:10–25; Luke 8:9–18).[6]

When the disciples seemed reluctant to confess their bewilderment, then Jesus often would have to take the initiative in clearing up the problem. The story of the rich young ruler is a typical incident. After Jesus dealt with him rather sternly, and the young ruler went away sorrowful because he loved his riches more than the Kingdom of God, Jesus turned to his disciples and said: "It is hard for a rich man to enter into the kingdom of heaven" (Matt. 19:23; cf., Mark 10:23; Luke 18:24). "The disciples were amazed at his words" (Mark 10:24). This led to an extended conversation in which Jesus explained the reason for his approach to this good moral man, while also using the opportunity to apply the principle to their own profession of faith (Mark 10:24–31; Matt. 19:24–20:16; Luke 18:25–30).

The Principle in Focus

The method of Jesus here was more than a continuous sermon; it was an object lesson as well. This was the secret of his influence in teaching. He did not ask anyone to do or be anything which first he had not demonstrated in his own life, thereby not only proving its workability, but also its relevance to his mission in life. And this he was able to do because he was constantly with his disciples. His training classes were never dismissed. Everything which he said and did was a personal lesson in reality, and since the disciples were there to notice it, they were learning practically every moment of their waking day.

How else will his way ever be learned? It is good to tell people what we mean, but it is infinitely better to show them. People are looking for a demonstration, not an explanation.

The Principle Applied Today

When it is all boiled down, those of us who are seeking to train people must be prepared to have them follow us, even as we follow Christ (1 Cor. 11:1). We are the exhibit (Phil. 3:17f.; 1 Thess. 2:7, 8; 2 Tim. 1:13). They will do those things which they hear and see in us (Phil. 4:9). Given time, it is possible through this kind of leadership to impart our way of living to those who are constantly with us.

We must take this truth to our lives. There can be no shirking or evading of our personal responsibility to show the way to those we are training, and this revelation must include the practical outworking in life of the deeper realities of the Spirit.

This is the Master's method, and nothing else will ever suffice to train others to do his work.

It makes us vulnerable, of course. We are not perfect like our Lord, and those persons to whom we open our lives will come to see our many shortcomings. But let them also see a readiness to confess our sins when we understand the error of our way. Let them hear us apologize to those we have wronged. Our weaknesses need not impair discipleship when shining through them is a transparent sincerity to follow Christ.

Yet, as we know, mere knowledge is not enough. There comes a time for action. To disregard this privilege can nullify all that has been acquired in the process of learning. Indeed, knowledge unapplied to living can become a stumbling-stone to further truth. No one better understood this than the Master. He was training men to do a job, and when they knew enough to get started, he saw to it that they did something about it. The application of this principle is so pronounced that it needs to be considered as another part of his strategy of conquest through trained and spiritually alert men.

I will make you fishers of men
Matthew 4:19

6

Delegation

He Assigned Them Work

Jesus was always building his ministry for the time when his disciples would have to take over his work, and go out into the world with the redeeming gospel. This plan was progressively made clear as they followed him.

The patience with which Jesus brought this out to his disciples reflects on his consideration for their ability to learn. He was never premature in his insistence on action. The first invitation to the disciples to follow him said nothing about going out and evangelizing the world, although this was his plan from the beginning. His method was to get the disciples into a vital experience with God, and to show them how he worked, before telling them they had to do it.

On the other hand, Jesus did not discourage their spontaneous reactions to bear witness to their faith, and in fact, he seemed delighted that they wanted to bring others to know what they had found. Andrew got Peter, Philip found Nathanael, Matthew invited his friends to a feast in his house—and Jesus responded to these new introductions with gladness. It is well, also, to note that on several occasions Jesus specifically asked those who were helped by his ministry to say something about it to others. However, in none of these early instances is the real purpose of their life of witnessing made a matter of explicit command.

He used his disciples in other ways to help along his work, such as caring for the manual burdens of getting food and arranging accommodations for the group as they followed him. He also let them baptize some people who were aroused by his message (John 4:2).[1] Outside of this, however, it is rather startling to observe in the Gospels that these early disciples really did not do much more than watch Jesus work for a year or more. He kept the vision before them by his activity, and in his call again to the four fishermen he reminded them that following him they were to be fishers of men (Mark 1:17; Matt. 4:19; Luke 5:10), but it does not seem that they did much about it. For that matter, even after they were formally ordained to the ministry a few months later (Mark 3:14–19; Luke 6:13–16), they still showed no evidence of doing any evangelistic work on their own. This observation perhaps should cause us to be more patient with new converts who follow us.

But as Jesus was beginning his third general tour of Galilee (Mark 6:6; Matt. 9:35), he doubtless realized that the time had come when his disciples could join him more directly in the work. They had seen enough at least to get started. They needed now to put into practice what they had seen their Master do. So "he called unto him the twelve, and began to send them forth" (Mark 6:7; cf., Matt. 10:5; Luke 9:1, 2). Like a mother eagle teaching her young to fly by pushing them out of the nest, Jesus pushed his disciples out into the world to try their own wings.

Briefing Instructions

Before letting them go, however, Jesus gave them some briefing instructions regarding their mission. What he said to them on this occasion is very important to this study because, in a sense, he outlined for them explicitly what he had been teaching implicitly all the time.

He first reaffirmed his purpose for their lives. They were to go and "preach the Kingdom of God, and to heal the sick" (Luke 9:1, 2; cf., Matt. 10:1; Mark 6:7). Nothing was new in this commission, but it did serve to further clarify their task. However, their new instructions did emphasize more the immediacy of their task with the announcement that the "kingdom was at hand" (Matt. 10:7). It also spelled out more completely the scope of their authority by telling them not only to heal, but to "cleanse the lepers, cast out devils, and raise the dead" (Matt. 10:8).

But Jesus did not leave it at this. He went on to tell them who to see first. "Go not into any way of the Gentiles, and enter not into any city of the Samaritans; but go rather to the lost sheep of the house of Israel" (Matt. 10:5, 6). It was as though Jesus was telling his disciples to go where they would find the most susceptible audience to hear their message. This is the way that Jesus proceeded in his ministry, although as time went on he did not confine himself to it. Since kinsmen were those most like them in cultural and religious background, it is only natural that they start with them. Interestingly enough, a few months later, when the seventy are sent out, this parting injunction was not repeated, perhaps indicating it was time then to go beyond these natural ties in pressing the claims of Christ.

As to their support, they were to trust God to supply their needs. They were told to render their services freely, remembering how they had also freely received from their Lord

(Matt. 10:8). Consequently, Jesus instructed them not to burden themselves unnecessarily with a lot of excess baggage and provisions (Matt. 10:9, 10; Mark 6:8, 9; Luke 9:3). As they were faithful to God, he would see to it that they were supplied their needs. "The laborer is worthy of his food" (Matt. 10:10).

Follow His Method

The plan of Jesus is even more specific to his disciples in his instructions to find some friendly person in each town they visited, and there live as long as they continued their evangelistic work in the area. "Into whatsoever city or village ye shall enter, search out who in it is worthy; and there abide till ye go forth" (Matt. 10:11; cf., Mark 6:10; Luke 9:4). In effect, the disciples were told to concentrate their time on the most promising individuals in each town who would thereby be able to follow up their work after they had gone. This was to receive priority over everything else. In fact, if they could not find someone who would take them in, they were specifically instructed to shake off the dust on their feet as a testimony against them. It would be "more tolerable for the land of Sodom and Gomorrah in the day of judgment, than for that city" (Matt. 10:14, 15; cf., Luke 9:5; Mark 6:11). This principle of establishing a beachhead in a new place of labor by connecting with a potentially key follow-up leader is not to be minimized. Jesus had lived by it with his own disciples, and he expected them to do the same. His whole plan of evangelism depended on it, and those places which refused the disciples opportunity to practice this principle actually brought the judgment of utter darkness on themselves.

Expect Hardship

The fact that some people would refuse the disciples' ministry only accentuated Jesus' warning of the treatment they could expect to receive. "Beware of men: for they will scourge you; yea and before governors and kings shall ye be brought for my sake, for a testimony to them and to the Gentiles" (Matt. 10:17, 18). This was only natural, since "a disciple is not above his master, or a servant above his Lord" (Matt. 10:24). The rulers had called Jesus Beelzebub, and those of his household could not expect any less abuse (Matt. 10:25). This was to say again that his way was contrary to the accepted pattern of worldly wisdom. Therefore they would be hated of all men (Matt. 10:22, 23). Nevertheless, Jesus told them to "fear not." God would never desert them. And though their witness could endanger their lives, the Holy Spirit would enable them to meet emergencies (Matt. 10:20, 21). No matter what happened to them, Jesus assured them that everyone who confessed him before men would be remembered before his Father in heaven (Matt. 10:32).

One cannot help being impressed with the realistic way that Jesus never let his followers underestimate the strength of the enemy, nor the natural resistance of self-serving people to his redeeming gospel. The disciples were not looking for trouble. Indeed, his admonition to them to be "as wise as serpents, and harmless as doves" (Matt. 10:16) underscored the need for propriety and tactfulness, but in spite of all their precautions, the fact remained that the world was not likely to receive the disciples with favor when they faithfully preached the gospel. They were sent "as sheep in the midst of wolves" (Matt. 10:16).

A Dividing Gospel

It is significant, too, that Jesus reminded them of the decisive nature of the gospel invitation. There could be no compromise with sin, and for this reason, anyone holding out on God was sure to be disturbed by their preaching. They were not hand-shaking emissaries maintaining the status quo of complacency. Rather Jesus said: "Think not that I came to send peace on the earth: I came not to send peace, but a sword. For I came to set a man at a variance against his father, and the daughter against her mother, and the daughter-in-law against her mother-in-law; and a man's foes shall be they of his own household. He that loveth father or mother more than me is not worthy of me: and he that loveth son or daughter more than me is not worthy of me. And he that doth not take his cross and follow after me, is not worthy of me" (Matt. 10:34–38). If the disciples had any notions prior to this time about the easy nature of their work, they were certainly dispelled now. They were going forth with a revolutionary gospel, and when it was obeyed, it effected a revolutionary change in people and their society.

One with Christ

The point Jesus made in all these instructions was that the mission of his disciples was not different in principle or method from his own. He began by giving them his own authority and power to do his work (Mark 6:7; Matt. 10:1; Luke 9:1), and he closed by assuring them that what they were doing was as though he was doing it himself. "He that receiveth you receiveth me, and he that receiveth me receiveth him that sent me" (Matt. 10:40; cf., John 13:20). Think of this identity! The disciples were to be the actual representatives of Christ as they went forth. So clear was this association that if someone even gave a child a cup of cold water in the name of a disciple, that act of mercy would be rewarded (Matt. 10:42).

Two by Two

These were the instructions that Jesus gave to his disciples. But before they went out, he teamed them up in pairs (Mark 6:7).[2] Doubtless this plan was intended to provide for his disciples' needed companionship along the way. Together they could help one another, and when adverse circumstances greeted them as surely often would be the case, they could still find solace among themselves. It reflects again the characteristic concern of Jesus for togetherness.

"And they departed, and went throughout the villages, preaching the Gospel, and healing everywhere" (Luke 9:6; cf., Mark 6:12). The little group of disciples were finally started in the active ministry of Christ on their own.

Of course, this was no excuse for Jesus to neglect his own work. He never asked anyone to do something which he was unwilling to do. So as the disciples went out, the Master likewise "departed thence to teach and preach in their cities" (Matt. 11:1).

The Mission of Seventy

Not many months after this "seventy others" were sent out again two by two to witness for their Lord (Luke 10:1). It is not known for sure just who these other disciples were, but the indications are that they included the Twelve. The size of the group also indicates that this was due in measure to the increased activity of the Twelve in witnessing for Christ.

Again the instructions given to this larger group were essentially the same as those delivered earlier to the Twelve (Luke 10:2–16). One addition in this new commission was the reminder that they were going "into every city and place, whither he himself was about to come" (Luke 10:1). That is, the disciples were forerunners for their Lord, setting things up for his ministry. This detail had been impressed on them a few weeks before while they were on a trip to Samaria (Luke 9:52), so actually it was not something of which they had no previous knowledge. It merely indicated again that they all were to practice what they had learned to be their Master's strategy of evangelism.

Postresurrection Commands

The principle of giving evangelistic work assignments to his disciples was conclusively demonstrated just before Jesus returned to heaven after his crucifixion and resurrection. On at least four occasions as he met with his disciples he told them to go out and do his work. It was first mentioned to the disciples, with the exception of Thomas, on that first Easter evening as they were assembled in the upper room. After Jesus had showed the astonished disciples his nail-scarred hands and feet (Luke 24:38–40), and had partaken of the meal with them (Luke 24:41–43), he then said: "Peace be unto you: as the Father hath sent me, even so send I you" (John 20:21), whereupon Jesus assured them again of the promise and authority of the Holy Spirit to do the work.

A little later as Jesus had breakfast with his disciples by the Sea of Tiberias, he told Peter three times to feed his sheep (John 21:15–17). This admonition was interpreted to the big fisherman as the proof of his love to the Master.

On a mountain in Galilee he gave his Great Commission to, not only the eleven disciples (Matt. 28:16), but also to the whole church numbering then about five hundred brethren (1 Cor. 15:6). It was a clear proclamation of his strategy of world conquest. "All authority hath been given unto me in heaven and in earth. Go ye therefore, and make disciples of all the nations, baptizing them into the name of the Father and of the Son and of the Holy Ghost, teaching them to observe all things whatsoever I commanded you: and lo, I am with you always, even unto the end of the world" (Matt. 28:18–20; cf., Mark 16:15–18).

Finally, before he ascended back to the Father, Jesus went over the whole thing again with his disciples for the last time, showing them how things had to be fulfilled while he was with them (Luke 24:44, 45). His suffering and death, as well as his resurrection from the dead the third day, was all according to schedule (Luke 24:46). Jesus went on to show his disciples "that repentance and remission of sin should be preached in his name unto all nations, beginning from Jerusalem" (Luke 24:47). And for the fulfillment of this divine purpose, the disciples were no less a part than their Master. They were to be the human instruments announcing the good tidings, and the Holy Spirit was to be God's personal empowerment for their mission. "Ye shall receive power when the Holy Ghost is come upon you: and ye shall be my witnesses both in Jerusalem, and in all Judea and Samaria, and unto the uttermost part of the earth" (Acts 1:8; cf., Luke 24:48, 49).

The Principle Is Clear

Clearly Jesus did not leave the work of evangelism subject to human impression or convenience. To his disciples it was a definite command, perceived by impulse at the beginning of their discipleship, but progressively clarified in their thinking as they followed him, and finally spelled out in no uncertain terms. No one who followed Jesus very far could escape this conclusion. It was so then; it is so today.

Christian disciples are sent men and women—sent out in the same work of world evangelism to which the Lord was sent, and for which he gave his life. Evangelism is not an optional accessory to our life. It is the heartbeat of all that we are called to be and do. It is the commission of the church which gives meaning to all else that is undertaken in the name of Christ. With this purpose clearly in focus, everything which is done and said has glorious fulfillment of God's redemptive purpose—educational institutions, social programs, hospitals, church meetings of any kind—everything done in the name of Christ has its justification in fulfilling this mission.

The Principle Applied Today

But it is not enough to make this an ideal. It must be given tangible expression by those who are following the Savior. The best way to be sure that this is done is to give practical work assignments and expect them to be carried out. This gets people started, and where they already have seen their work demonstrated in the life of their teacher there is no reason why the assignment cannot be completed. When the church takes this lesson to heart, and gets down to business with evangelism, then those in the pews will soon start moving out for God.

However, the fact that one starts the work is no assurance that he or she will keep it up. Once inertia is overcome, it is still necessary to keep one moving and going in the right direction. Certainly the assignments that Jesus gave his followers, at least at first, were no discharge from his school of training. They had much more to learn before they could be considered ready for graduation, and until that time came, he had no intention of turning them loose from his personal direction. His concern at this point was so explicit and his method of dealing with it so pronounced that it needs to be considered as another step in his strategy of ultimate victory.

Do ye not yet perceive?
Mark 8:17

7

Supervision

He Kept Check on Them

Jesus made it a point to meet with his disciples following their tours of service to hear their reports and to share with them the blessedness of his ministry in doing the same thing. In this sense, one might say that his teaching rotated between instruction and assignment. What time he was with them, he was helping them to understand the reason for some previous action or getting them ready for some new experience. His questions, illustrations, warnings, and admonitions were calculated to bring out those things that they needed to know in order to fulfill his work, which was the evangelization of the world.

Accordingly, not long after the Twelve were sent out, they gathered themselves "together with Jesus" to tell "what things they had done" (Mark 6:30; Luke 9:10). It would appear from the Bible that this reunion was prearranged, and hence, the initial solo excursion of the disciples was merely a field assignment as they continued their training with the Master.

The regrouping of the disciples following their evangelistic tour, of course, provided them some needed rest in body and soul. As to how long the disciples had been out, the Scripture does not say. Perhaps a few days, even a week. The time element here is not the important thing. What does matter though, as the record shows, is that after the disciples were sent out to work, they were expected to share their experiences, later, with the group.

Similarly, after the seventy went out, Jesus called them back to report on their work during the visitation. "And the seventy returned with joy, saying, Lord, even the devils are subject unto us in thy name" (Luke 10:17). On the previous mission of the Twelve, no mention is made of any spectacular success in their work, but on this occasion they had a rousing report of triumph. Perhaps the difference was the additional experience which the disciples had gained.

Nothing could have given Jesus more joy than this. Visualizing the victory ultimately assured by their work, Jesus said: "I beheld Satan falling as lightning from heaven" (Luke 10:18). "In that same hour he rejoiced in the Holy Spirit" and then lifted up his voice in praise to God for what had been done (Luke 10:21, 22). This was what Jesus had been working for all these long months, and now he was beginning to see his labors show fruit. Yet, to show how Jesus was alert to make experiences teach truth, even this occasion was used to caution the disciples against pride in their accomplishments. As he put it, "Howbeit in this rejoice not, that the spirits are subject unto you; but rejoice that your names are written in heaven" (Luke 10:20).

Continuous Review and Application

What is seen here so vividly in these checkup sessions following the disciples' visitation merely brings into bold relief a strategy of Jesus throughout his ministry. As he reviewed some experience which the disciples had he would bring out some practical application of it to their lives.

Take, as an illustration, the way he responded to the futile efforts of some of his disciples to heal an afflicted boy. This incident occurred while Jesus was on the Mount of Trans-figuration, with Peter, James, and John. In his absence, the other disciples had tried to heal a demon-possessed boy brought to them by the father. The case was too much for their faith, and when Jesus returned to see how things were, he found the distraught father with the sick child having a fit before the helpless disciples. Jesus, of course, took care of the boy, but he did not let the occasion pass without giving the frustrated disciples a much needed lesson on how they, through more prayer and fasting, should have laid hold upon God's faithfulness (Mark 9:17–29; Matt. 17:14–20; Luke 9:37–43).

Or, again, think of the way he recalled their part in feed-ing the multitude to impress on them his power to do all things, while also teaching them a vital lesson concerning spiritual discernment (Mark 6:30–44; 7:31–8:9, 13–21; Matt. 14:13–21; 15:29–38; Luke 9:10–17; John 6:1–13). It came about as they were going across the sea of Galilee in a boat immediately following the Master's severe denunciation of the chronic sign-seeking attitude of the religious sects of his day (Mark 8:10–12; Matt. 15:39–16:4). Jesus, doubtless feel-ing a great heaviness because of the incident on the other side of the lake, turned to his disciples and said: "Take heed, beware of the leaven of the Pharisees." But the spiritually dull disciples, growing hungry for food, and having only one loaf of bread with them, thought that they should not buy bread from these unbelieving people, and therefore wondered where their next meal was coming from. Realizing that they had missed completely the spiritual lesson of his remarks intended to warn them against unbelief, Jesus said: "O ye of little faith, why reason ye among yourselves, because ye have no bread? Do ye not yet perceive, neither understand? Have ye your heart hardened? Having eyes, see ye not? And having ears, hear ye not? And do ye not remember? When I brake the five loaves among the five thousand, how many baskets full of broken pieces took ye up?" The disciples answered, "Twelve" (Mark 16:8; Mark 8:17–19).

Doubtless this brought clearly to mind that day when the disciples seated the multitudes for dinner, and then saw Jesus perform the miracle of the loaves.[1] They remembered, too, how he employed them to distribute the provisions so that everybody had enough, and then to gather up what was left. Indeed, it was a vivid recollection, for each one of the Twelve had a basket full of food when it was all over. Similarly, they remembered how that they had seven baskets left over from feeding the four thousand. With this evidence of Jesus' miraculous power there could be no doubt about his ability to feed them with their loaf of bread if it was necessary. "Then understood they that he bade them not beware of the leaven of bread, but of the teaching of the Pharisees and Sadducees" (Matt. 16:12).

Lessons on Patience

One of the most penetrating of the Lord's correctional lectures following the disciples' activity was in connection with their attitude toward others in the work who were not members of the apostolic company. It seems that in the course of their travels they had run across some people casting out demons in Jesus' name, but since these persons were not of their denomination, the disciples had severely rebuked them for it (Mark 9:38; Luke 9:49). Doubtless Jesus' disciples felt they were doing the right thing, but when it was reported to the Master, he felt constrained to give them an extended discourse on the dangers of discouraging any sincere work on his behalf (Mark 9:39–50; Matt. 18:6–14). "Forbid him not," Jesus said, "for he that is not against you is for you" (Luke 9:50). Then making his point apply more generally to all innocent people, especially children, he went on to say, "Whosoever shall cause one of these little ones that believe on me to stumble, it were better for him if a great millstone were hanged about his neck, and he were cast into the sea" (Mark 9:42). "It is not the will of your Father which is in heaven, that one of these little ones should perish" (Matt. 18:14).

On another excursion, the disciples encountered some resistance to their work while on an assignment for their Lord in Samaria. Reacting impulsively to destroy the people, they wanted to call down fire from heaven (Luke 9:51–54). But Jesus, who was standing nearby, "turned and rebuked them," adding, "Ye know not what manner of spirit ye are of. For the Son of man came not to destroy men's lives, but to save them" (Luke 9:55, 56). And then showing his disciples how they might solve this kind of problem, "they went to another village" (Luke 9:56).

The Principle Observed

Many other illustrations could be cited to show how Jesus checked up on the actions and reactions of his disciples as they faced various difficult situations. He kept after them constantly, giving them increasingly more attention as his ministry on earth came to a close. He would not let them rest in success or in failure. No matter what they did, there was always more to do and to learn. He rejoiced in their success, but nothing less than world conquest was his goal, and to that end he always superintended their efforts.[2]

Here was on-the-job training at its best. Jesus would let his followers have some experience or make some observation of their own, and then he would use this as a starting point to teach a lesson of discipleship. The fact that they tried to do his work, even though they may have failed at it, gave them greater awareness of their deficiencies, and hence they were more disposed to the Master's correction. Moreover, their encounter with life situations enabled Jesus to pinpoint his teaching on specific needs and to spell it out in the concrete terms of practical experience. We always appreciate an education more after we have had the opportunity to apply what we have learned.

The important thing about all this supervisionary work of Jesus was that he kept the disciples going on toward the goal he had set for them. He did not expect more from his disciples than they could do, but he did expect their best, and this he expected always to be improved as they grew in knowledge and grace. His plan of teaching, by example, assignment, and constant checkup, was calculated to bring out the best that was in them.

The Principle Applied Today

No less patient yet determined supervision is needed today among those who are seeking to train others for evangelism. We dare not assume that the work will be done merely because we have shown a willing worker how to do it, and then sent him or her out with a glowing expectation of results. Innumerable things could happen to frustrate and sidetrack the work, and unless these matters are dealt with realistically by competent and understanding people, the worker may easily become discouraged and defeated. Likewise, many experiences of grace which bring delight to the soul need to be clarified and deepened as their meaning is interpreted in the light of the total world mission of Christ. It is thus crucial that those engaging in the work of evangelism have personal supervision and guidance until such time as they are matured enough to carry on alone.

We must always remember, too, that the goal is world conquest. We dare not let a lesser concern capture our strategy of the moment. All too many times one has been brought to the place of service only to be discharged with no further training or inspiration. The result is that the activity becomes localized in a feverish round of excitement. There is no growth. The potential ability resident in the worker is not developed, and before long a promising leader is spoiled for want of supervision. Success is lost on the eve of victory. What once looked so good eventually becomes a stumbling stone to the best.

Undoubtedly much of our effort for the Kingdom is dissipated for this reason. We fail, not because we do not try to do something, but because we let our little efforts become an excuse for not doing more. The result is that we lose by default the advantage of years of hard work and sacrifice.

When will we learn the lesson of Christ not to be satisfied merely with the firstfruits of those who are sent out to witness? Disciples must be brought to maturity. There can be no substitute for total victory, and our field is the world. We have not been called to hold the fort, but to storm the heights. It is in this light that the final step in Jesus' strategy of evangelism can be understood.

Go and bring forth fruit
John 15:16

8

Reproduction

He Expected Them to Reproduce

Jesus intended for the disciples to produce his likeness in and through the church being gathered out of the world. Thus his ministry in the Spirit would be duplicated many-fold by his ministry in the lives of his disciples. Through them and others like them it would continue to expand in an ever-enlarging circumference until the multitudes might know in a similar way the opportunity which they had known with the Master. By this strategy the conquest of the world was only a matter of time and their faithfulness to his plan.

Jesus had built into his disciples the structure of a church that would challenge and triumph over all the powers of death and hell. It had started small like a grain of mustard seed, but it would grow in size and strength until it became a tree "greater than all the herbs" (Matt. 13:32; cf., Mark 4:32; Luke 13:18, 19). Jesus did not expect that everyone would be saved (he recognized realistically the rebellion of men in spite of grace), but he did foresee the day when the gospel of salvation in his name would be proclaimed convincingly to every creature. Through that testimony his church militant would someday be the church universal even as it would become the church triumphant.

It was not going to be an easy conquest. Many would suffer persecution and martyrdom in the battle. Yet no matter how great the trials through which his people would pass, and how many temporal skirmishes were lost in the struggle, the ultimate victory was certain. His church would win in the end.[1] Nothing could permanently prevail against it "or be strong to its detriment, or hold out against it" (Matt. 16:18, *Amplified New Testament*).

Victory Through Witnessing

This incredible confidence in the future was based on his knowledge of those who worshiped him in the present. He knew that his disciples had learned at least the essence of his glory. Peter, the spokesman for the band, had summed it up in his affirmation to Jesus: "Thou art the Christ, the Son of the living God" (Matt. 16:16; cf., Mark 8:29; Luke 9:20). Here was a truth indestructible, and it was on this foundation that Jesus envisioned how his victory would be won, as he replied: "Thou art Peter, and upon this rock I will build my church" (Matt. 16:18).

The force of these words indicates the significance of human initiative in bringing it to pass. Irrespective of the excitement aroused by the ecclesiastical overtones of the passage, we should agree, at least, that Jesus' words were addressed to a person who personally had made an affirmation of faith in his Lord.[2] Indeed, this realization of his Master being the very Son of God was not something which Peter had worked up himself, as Jesus made so clear (Matt. 16:17). Nevertheless, the experience of that revelation in his life was quite definitely located in his "flesh and blood," and through the faithful expression of that fact to others, the church of Christ was destined to triumph.[3] How could it perish? The apostle's faith in the living Christ was so imbedded in his life that it had solidified into a rock—a rock which Peter recognized to be his Lord, "the chief cornerstone," on which all believers were "living stones" in the construction of his church (1 Peter 2:4–8; cf., Eph. 2:20–22).[4]

However, we must not fail to see the direct relation between bearing witness of Christ and the ultimate victory over the world. One cannot come without the other. Bringing these two dynamic facts together by the power of the Holy Spirit is the climactic genius of Jesus' strategy of evangelism.

The Principle Observed

It all comes back to his disciples. They were the vanguard of his enveloping movement. "Through their word" he expected others to believe in him (John 17:20), and these in turn to pass the word along to others, until in time the world might know who he was and what he came to do (John 17:21, 23). His whole evangelistic strategy—indeed, the fulfillment of his very purpose in coming into the world, dying on the cross, and rising from the grave—depended on the faithfulness of his chosen disciples to this task. It did not matter how small the group was to start with so long as they reproduced and taught their disciples to reproduce. This was the way his church was to win—through the dedicated lives of those who knew the Savior so well that his Spirit and method constrained them to tell others. As simple as it may seem, this was the way the gospel would conquer. He had no other plan.

The Test of His Ministry

Here was the acid test. Would his disciples carry on his work after he had gone? Or what might be even more to the

point, could they do as good a job without his bodily supervision as they could with it? This may sound like asking too
much, but the fact is that until this point was reached in their
Christian nurture, Jesus from a purely human point of view
could never be sure that his investment in their lives would
pay off for the Kingdom. If the disciples failed to impart his
Spirit and method to others who would keep this work going,
then his ministry with them all these years would soon come
to nought.

No wonder Jesus so indelibly impressed on his disciples
the necessity and inevitability of life reproducing its kind. An
illustration of this was the parable of the vine and the branches
(John 15:1–17). Here in one of the most simple yet profound analogies of the Lord, Christ explained that the purpose of both the vine (himself) and the branches (believers
in him) was to bear fruit. Hence, any branch that did not
yield produce was cut off by the husbandman—it was worth-
less. What is more, those branches which did produce were
pruned by the husbandman that they might yield more fruit
(John 15:2). It was clear that the life-sustaining power of the
vine was not to be bestowed endlessly on lifeless branches.
Any branch that lived on the vine had to produce to survive
for that was its intended nature. Jesus then made the application to his disciples. As surely as they were participants in
his life, even so they would bear his fruit (John 15:5, 8), and
furthermore, their fruit would remain (John 15:16).[5] A bar-
ren Christian is a contradiction. A tree is known by its fruit.

This principle was emphasized time and time again
throughout his ministry. It was seen as the inevitable reward
of his own sacrifice for the world (John 12:24; cf., 17:19). It
was made the distinguishing work of those who did the will
of his Father in heaven (Matt. 7:16–23; Luke 6:43–45). It
was interpreted as the wages given to his disciples for their
work in the harvest (John 4:36–38). It was recognized as

that which was denied those who "let the cares of the world, the deceitfulness of riches, and the lusts of other things" choke out the Word of God planted in their hearts (Mark 4:18–20; Matt. 13:22, 23; Luke 8:14, 15). It was observed as the thing lacking in the lives of the Sadducees and Pharisees which made them so wretched in his sight (Matt. 3:7, 8; 12:33, 34; Luke 13:6–9). In various ways, and among all kinds of people, Jesus called men to evaluate the product of their lives. This was the revelation of what they were. In fact, where fruitbearing is seen in its larger context of reproducing the Christ life in human personality, first in ourselves and then in others, practically everything which the Master said and did pointed to this principle.

The Great Commission

The Great Commission of Christ given to his church summed it up in the command to "make disciples of every creature" (Matt. 28:19). The word here indicates that the disciples were to go out into the world and win others who would come to be what they themselves were—disciples of Christ. This mission is emphasized even more when the Greek text of the passage is studied, and it is seen that the words *go, baptize,* and *teach* are all participles which derive their force from the one controlling verb "make disciples."[6] This means that the Great Commission is not merely to go to the ends of the earth preaching the gospel (Mark 16:15), nor to baptize a lot of converts into the name of the triune God, nor to teach them the precepts of Christ, but to "make disciples"—to build people like themselves who were so constrained by the commission of Christ that they not only followed, but also led others to follow his way. Only as disciples were made could the other activities of the commission fulfill their purpose.

Pray for Harvesters

Leadership was the emphasis. Jesus had already demonstrated by his own ministry that the deluded masses were ripe
for the harvest, but without spiritual shepherds to lead them,
how could they ever be won? "Pray ye therefore the Lord of
the harvest," Jesus reminded his disciples, "that he will send
forth laborers into his harvest" (Matt. 9:37, 38; cf., Luke
10:2). There is almost a note of desperation in these words—
a desperation wrung from the sense of the world's desperate
need of workers with them who cared for their souls. There
is no use to pray for the world. What good would it do? God
already loves them and has given his Son to save them. No,
there is no use to pray vaguely for the world. The world is
lost and blind in sin. The only hope for the world is for laborers to go to them with the gospel of salvation, and having
won them to the Savior, not to leave them, but to work with
them faithfully, patiently, painstakingly, until they become
fruitful Christians savoring the world about them with the
Redeemer's love.

The Principle Applied to Our Lives

Here finally is where we must all evaluate the contribution
that our life and witness is making to the supreme purpose of
him who is the Savior of the world. Are those who have followed us to Christ now leading others to him and teaching
them to make disciples like ourselves? Note, it is not enough
to rescue the perishing, though this is imperative; nor is it sufficient to build up newborn babes in the faith of Christ,
although this too is necessary if the firstfruit is to endure; in
fact, it is not sufficient just to get them out winning souls, as
commendable as this work may be. What really counts in the
ultimate perpetuation of our work is the faithfulness with

which our converts go out and make leaders out of their converts, not simply more followers. Surely we want to win our
generation for Christ, and to do it now, but this is not enough.
Our work is never finished until it has assured its continuation in the lives of those redeemed by the Evangel.

The test of any work of evangelism thus is not what is seen
at the moment, or in the conference report, but in the effectiveness with which the work continues in the next generation. Similarly the criteria on which a church should measure
its success is not how many new names are added to the roll
nor how much the budget is increased, but rather how many
Christians are actively winning souls and training them to
win the multitudes. The ultimate extent of our witness is what
matters, and for this reason values can be measured only by
eternity.

Is it not time that we all looked again at our lives and ministries from this perspective? As Dawson Trotman would say,
"Where are our men?"[7] What are they doing for God? Consider what it would mean to the future of the church if we
had only one true disciple now to show for our labors. Would
not this immediately double our influence? And suppose that
we made another like ourself, even as the first succeeded in
the same way. Would not this multiply our life four times
over? Theoretically, at least, in this manner of multiplication
our ministry alone would soon reach multitudes with the
gospel. That is, if that person we had called a disciple truly
followed in the steps of the Master.

Proved by the Church

We can be thankful that in those first disciples this was
done. They gave the gospel to the multitudes, but all the
while they were building up the fellowship of those who
believed. As the Lord added daily to the church such as were

saved, the apostles, like their Master, were developing men to reproduce their ministry to the ends of the earth. The Acts of the Apostles is really just the unfolding in the life of the growing church the principles of evangelism that have already been outlined here in the life of Christ.[8]

Suffice it to say that the early church proved that the Master's plan for world conquest worked. So great was the impact of their witness that before the century had passed the pagan society of the day had been shaken to its foundations and growing churches had been established in most centers of population. Had the momentum continued in the evangelistic outreach of the church that characterized its beginning, within a few centuries the multitudes of the world would have known the touch of the Master's hand.

Shortcuts Have Failed

But times changed, and gradually the simple way of Jesus' evangelism was forced into a new mold. Of course, adaptations of principle are always necessary in the light of changing circumstances, but somehow or other the principles themselves got confused in the desire to give the Evangel a new look. The costly principles of leadership development and reproduction seem to have been submerged beneath the easier strategy of mass recruitment. The nearsighted objective of popular recognition generally took precedence over the long-range goal of reaching the world, and the methods of evangelism employed by the church collectively and individually have reflected this same momentary outlook. Occasionally, as in times of great spiritual revival, the principles of Jesus' method have come to the fore, but to this observer of church history such periods have been short-lived and have never captured the imagination of the vast majority of churchmen. Jesus' plan has not been disavowed; it has just been ignored. It has been something to remember in venerating the past, but not to be taken seriously as a rule for conduct in the present.

The Issue Today

This is our problem of methodology today. Well-intended ceremonies, programs, organizations, commissions, and crusades of human ingenuity are trying valiantly to do a job that only can be done by people in the power of the Holy Spirit. This is not to depreciate these noble efforts, for without them the church could not function as she does. Nevertheless, unless the personal mission of the Master is vitally incorporated into the policy and fabric of all these plans, the church cannot function as she should.

When will we realize that evangelism is not done by something, but by someone? It is an expression of God's love, and God is a person. His nature, being personal, is only expressed through personality, first revealed fully in Christ, and now expressed through his Spirit in the lives of those yielded to him. Committees may help to organize and direct it, and to that end they certainly are needed, but the work itself is done by people reaching other people for Christ.

That is why we must say with E. M. Bounds that "men are God's method."[9] Until we have such people imbued with his Spirit and committed to his plan, none of our methods will work.

This is the new evangelism we need. It is not better methods, but better men and women who know their Redeemer from personal experience—men and women who see his vision and feel his passion for the world—men and women who are willing to be nothing so that he might be everything—men and women who want only for Christ to produce his life in and through them according to his own good pleasure. This finally is the way the Master planned for his objective to be realized on the earth, and where it is carried through by his strategy, the gates of hell cannot prevail against the evangelization of the world.

I am the Alpha and the Omega
Revelation 1:8

Epilogue
The Master and Your Plan

Life Has a Plan

What is the plan of your life? Everyone has to live by some plan. The plan is the organizing principle around which the aim of life is carried out. We may not be conscious of the plan in every action, or even know that we have a plan, but nonetheless our actions invariably unfold some kind of a pattern at the center of things.

When we actually get right down to it, and try to see our objective and how we are going about to achieve it, what we discover may not be very satisfying. But an honest appraisal should cause us all to be more concerned for our calling, at least for those who believe Jesus' way is the rule by which every action should be tested.

It might well be that some cherished plans of our own making may have to be redirected, or perhaps abandoned altogether. Equally agonizing may be the adjustment of the congregation to the Master's view of the ministry. In all probability our whole concept of success will have to be reevaluated. Nevertheless, if the principles outlined here have any validity at all, they should be understood as guidelines for action. It is only as they are applied to the everyday work of living now that they have any real significance for our lives. To regard them as true means that they must be relevant.

Methods Will Vary

Every one of us then should be seeking some way to incorporate the wisdom of Jesus' strategy into our own preferred method of evangelism.[1] Not everyone will be led to adopt the same ritual or organization of procedure, nor should we want everyone to fit into the same mold. Variety is in the very structure of the universe, and any method that God is pleased to use is a good method, though this does not exclude the possibility of improvement in our way of doing it. The Master gives us an outline to follow, but he expects us to work out the details according to local circumstances and traditions. This demands every bit of resourcefulness that we have. New and bold approaches will need to be tried as situations change, and not everything tried will work. A person unwilling to fail in the determination to find some way to get the job done will never get started, nor will the one afraid to try and try again make much progress.

The Priority of People

But whatever the particular form our methodology takes, Jesus' life would teach us that finding and training people to reach people must have priority. The multitudes cannot know the gospel unless they have a living witness. Merely giving them an explanation will not suffice. The wandering masses of the world must have a demonstration of what to believe—they must have a mentor who will stand among them and say, "Follow me, I know the way." Here then is where all our plans must focus. No matter how spiritual our emphasis might otherwise be, the enduring relevance of all that we do will depend on how well this mission is fulfilled.

Yet we must realize that the kind of energy that Christ needs does not happen by accident. It requires deliberate planning and concentrated effort. If we are to train people, we must work for them. We must seek them. We must win them. Above all, we must pray for them. Some are already in positions of authority in the church. Others are yet among those waiting to receive an invitation to come to Christ. But wherever they are, they must be reached and trained to become effective witnesses of our Lord.

Begin with a Few

We should not expect a great number to begin with, nor should we desire it. The best work is always done with a few. Better to give a year or so to one or two people who learn what it means to conquer for Christ than to spend a lifetime with a congregation just keeping the program going. Nor does it matter how small or inauspicious the beginning may be; what counts is that those to whom we do give priority in our life learn to give it away.

This does not mean that we are the only persons involved in the discipling process. Other people also are impacting their lives—moms, dads, wives, husbands, children, church workers, teachers, friends of all kinds—and their witness, both positive and negative, will have its effect. But for a period of time, we may be the most decisive influence on their Christian maturity.

In a deeper sense, of course, Christ is the leader, not ourselves. Let this be absolutely clear. There is no place in discipleship for any authoritarian role of a master guru. So keep the focus on Jesus. He commands through the Spirit and the

Word. In subjection to him, disciple and discipler alike learn at his feet.

Stay Together

The only realistic way to effect this is by being together. If our followers are to see through us what they are to become, we must be with them. This is the essence of the plan—to let them see us in action so as to feel our vision and to know how it relates to daily experience. Evangelism thus becomes to them an intimately practical thing that has ramifications in everything else. It is seen as a way of life, not a theological dogma. What is more, by being with us, their own involvement in the work is inevitable.

Give Them Time

A plan like this, of course, is going to take time. Anything worthwhile does. But with a little forethought we can plan to do many things together which we would have to do anyway, such as visitation, going to conferences, getting recreation, and even having devotions together. Thus the time it takes to be together need not be overwhelming. Likewise, if we are alert, most of the time our disciples could be with us while we are serving others, and in fact, helping us in our larger outreach.

Group Meetings

To give a little stability to this system, however, it may be necessary to arrange special times when the group, or part of it, can meet together with us. During these informal gatherings we can study the Bible, pray, and in general share with one another our deepest burdens and desires. It is not necessary to broadcast what is being done, or even at first to tell the group what our ultimate plan is, but just let the meetings grow out of the common need for fellowship. In turn the group can work out its own particular discipline within the framework of the church.

This group idea is being rediscovered in many places today. As such it probably represents one of the most hopeful signs of awakening on the horizon. In all walks of life and within every kind of church connection little spiritual organisms are springing up, some of them struggling for direction, some off on a tangent, but on the whole, the movement expressing a deep yearning in the heart of people for the realities of Christian experience. Since they are not bound by tradition or fixed rules from without, there naturally is a wide difference in the emphasis and form these cells take, but the principle of close, disciplined fellowship within the group is common to most. It is this principle at the center which makes the method so conducive to growth, and for that reason all of us would do well to utilize it in our ministry with men and women.[2]

In this connection, it is not without great significance that the leading evangelist in the world today, Billy Graham, recognizes the tremendous potential of this plan when used properly in the church. In response to the question, "If you were a pastor of a large church in a principal city, what would be your plan of action?" Mr. Graham replied: "I think one of the first things I would do would be to get a small group of eight or ten or twelve people around me that would meet a few hours a week and pay the price! It would cost them something in time and effort. I would share with them everything I have, over a period of years. Then I would actually have twelve ministers among the laypeople who in turn could take eight or ten or twelve more and teach them. I know one or two churches that are doing that, and it is revolutionizing the church. Christ, I think, set the pattern. He spent most of his time with twelve men. He didn't spend it with a great crowd. In fact, every time he had a great crowd it seems to me that there weren't too many results. The great results, it seems to me, came in his personal interview and in the time he spent with his twelve."[3] Here Mr. Graham is merely echoing the wisdom of Jesus' method.

Expect Something from Them

But it is not enough just to involve persons in some kind of group association, of which the church is but the larger expression. They must be given some way to express the things which they have learned. Unless opportunity is provided for this outreach, the group can stagnate in self-contentment, and eventually fossilize into nothing more than a mutual admiration society. We must keep our purpose clear. The times that we come apart from the world are not a release from the conflict, but only a strategic maneuver to gain more strength for the attack.

It is our business, then, to see to it that those with us are given something to do which requires the best that is in them. Everyone can do something.[4] First assignments might be normal, routine tasks, such as mailing letters, setting up a public address system for an outdoor service, or for that matter, merely letting them provide for our entertainment in their home. But gradually these responsibilities can be increased as they are able to do more. Those with a teaching gift could be utilized in the Sunday school. Before long we might conveniently assign them some pastoral work suited to their ability. Most anyone can call on the sick or visit in the hospital. Some might be encouraged to take over some speaking engagements or fill nearby pulpits. And, of course, everyone needs to be given some specific work by way of personal evangelism.[5]

Probably no more essential contribution can they make to the ministry of the church than in the area of follow-up of new Christians.[6] Here, they can fill an indispensable role of the ministry by getting with those who are still babes in Christ and leading them on in the same disciplines and in the same way that they have been taught. Those whom we train for this work thus become the key to the preservation of every evangelistic effort of the church,[7] not only in conserving the forward advance, but also in assuring its continuing outreach.

Keep Them Going

All of this is going to require a lot of supervision, both in the personal development of these people, and in their work with others. We will have to make it a practice to meet with them and hear how things are going. This will mean seeking them out where they are or counseling with them while they are with us in other activity. Questions which have arisen in their experience must be answered while the circumstances that occasioned the problem are still fresh in their mind. Faulty attitudes and reactions need to be detected early and dealt with decisively, as also offensive personal habits, unfounded prejudices, and anything else that would obstruct their priesthood with God and with others.

The main thing is to help them keep growing in grace and in knowledge. It might be wise in respect to our human memory to set up for ourselves a schedule of things to cover in the course of their training, and then to keep a record somewhere of their progress to be sure that nothing is left out. This is particularly necessary where we may be working with several people at the same time, with each person at a different level of experience. We will need to exercise patience, for their development very likely will be slow and encumbered with many setbacks. But as long as they are honestly seeking to know the truth, and are willing to follow it, they will some-day grow up to maturity in Christ.

Help Them Carry Their Burdens

What perhaps is the most difficult part of the whole process of training is that we must anticipate their problems and pre-pare them for what they will face. This is terribly hard to do, and it can become exasperating. It means that we can seldom put them out of our mind. Even when we are in our private meditations and study our disciples will still be in our prayers and dreams. But would a parent who loves his children want it any other way? We have to accept the burden of their imma-turity until such time as they can do it for themselves. To take the attitude, at least in the early stages of their development, that they can handle completely on their own whatever comes along is inviting disaster. We must be sensible. As their guardian and advisor we are responsible for teaching our spir-itual children how to live for the Master.

Let Them Carry On

Everything should be leading these chosen men and women to the day when they will assume by themselves a ministry in their own sphere of influence. As that time approaches each one should be well along in a training pro-gram with those won to Christ by his or her witness or who have been assigned to him or her for follow-up. Our strat-egy thus without their knowledge will have already been infused into their practice. However, not to leave it obscure, before withdrawing our supervision we should explain to them explicitly what has been our plan from the beginning. They need to have it clearly in mind so that they can mea-sure their lives by it and also impart it to those that they are seeking to help.

Spiritual Experience Above All

The crucial thing, of course, is their own spiritual experience. Before they should be turned loose from our control they need to be thoroughly established in the faith that overcomes the world. The devil, assisted by all the demons of hell, will seek to defeat them by every cunning device at his command. The world to which they are going lies under his evil spell. It will be a battle all the way. Every inch of progress will have to be won by conquest, for the enemy will never surrender. Nothing less than the infilling of the Spirit of Christ will be sufficient to meet the challenge. Unless they live in his communion, and go forth in his purity and power, they can easily be overwhelmed by the forces amassed against them, and all our work with them be nullified.

Everything that we have done then depends on the faithfulness of these workers. It does not matter how many people we enlist for the cause, but how many they conquer for Christ. That is why all along our emphasis must be on quality of life. If we get the right quality of leadership, the rest will follow; if we do not get it, the rest have nothing worth following.

The Price of Victory Comes High

Such a high standard of expectation is costly, to be sure. Probably many of those we start out with will think it too much and fall by the way. We might as well face it now. Christian service is demanding, and if people are going to be of any use for God, they must learn to seek first the Kingdom. Yes, there will be disappointments. Those who do come through, and go out to project our life into harvest fields, will be a source of increasing joy as the years go by.

We are not living primarily for the present. Our satisfaction is in knowing that in generations to come our witness for Christ will still be bearing fruit through them in an ever-widening cycle of reproduction to the ends of the earth and unto the end of time.

Is This Your Vision?

The world is desperately seeking someone to follow. That they will follow someone is certain, but will that person be one who knows the way of Christ, or will he or she be one like themselves leading them only on into greater darkness?

This is the decisive question of our plan of life. The relevance of all that we do waits on its verdict, and in turn, the destiny of the multitudes hangs in the balance.

Endnotes

Preface—The Master and His Plan

1. There are a number of books which treat various phases of the evangelistic message and methodology of Jesus. Among those which provide many helpful insights are the following: Raymond Calkins, *How Jesus Dealt with Man* (Nashville: Abingdon-Cokesbury Press, 1942); Allan Knight Chalmers, *As He Passed By* (New York: The Abingdon Press, 1939); Ozora Davis, *Meeting the Master* (New York: Association Press, 1917); F. V. McFatridge, *The Personal Evangelism of Jesus* (Grand Rapids: Zondervan, 1939); G. Campbell Morgan, *The Great Physician* (New York: Fleming H. Revell Co., 1937); L. R. Scarborough, *How Jesus Won Men* (New York: George H. Doran Co., 1926); John Calhoun Sligh, *Christ's Way of Winning Souls* (Nashville: Publishing House of the M. E. Church, South, 1909); John Smith, *The Magnetism of Christ* (London: Hodder and Stoughton, 1904); Mack Stokes, *The Evangelism of Jesus* (Nashville: Methodist Evangelistic Materials, 1960); Earnest Clyde Wareing, *The Evangelism of Jesus* (New York: The Abingdon Press, 1918); and Faris D. Whitesell, *Basic New Testament Evangelism* (Grand Rapids: Zondervan, 1949). In addition to these works which specifically treat evangelistic methods of Jesus, there are many more which give it particular attention in a chapter or two, such as R. W. Cooper, *Modern Evangelism* (New York: Fleming H. Revell, 1929), Chapter II; Charles G. Trumbull, *Taking Men Alive* (New York: Fleming H. Revell, 1927), Chapter IX; and S. A. Whitmer, *Galilean Fisherman* (Berne, Indiana: Life and Hope Publications, 1940), Chapter X. However, to a varying degree every work that treats the life or teachings of Christ will have some reference to his evange

117

listic methods, and many of these larger works will have the most complete discussion of individual cases to be found anywhere. Needless to say, there is no want of material in this field if one will only search it out. (Many of the books cited here and throughout this book are no longer in print and may be available only in seminary libraries. Those fortunate enough to find them will be richly rewarded through the insights of these respected scholars.)

2. A few of the more pertinent volumes and the pages relevant are: Walter Albeon Squires, *The Pedagogy of Jesus* (Philadelphia: Westminster, 1927), pp. 67–168; Norman E. Richardson, *The Christ of the Class Room* (New York: Macmillan, 1931), pp. 121–82; and J. M. Price, *Jesus the Teacher* (Nashville: Convention Press, 1954), pp. 31–60.

3. For example, helpful information relative to Jesus' strategy may be found in such well-known works as Samuel J. Andrews, *The Life of Our Lord*, reprint of 1891 ed. (Grand Rapids: Zondervan, 1954), pp. 121, 122; J. P. Lange, *The Life of the Lord Jesus Christ*, 4 vols., reprint (Grand Rapids: Zondervan, 1958), I, pp. 393–410; II, pp. 182–97; Alfred Edersheim, *The Life and Times of Jesus the Messiah*, 2 vols. (New York: E. R. Herrick & Co., 1886), I, pp. 472–77; David Smith, *The Days of His Flesh* (London: Hodder & Stoughton, 1905), pp. 157–67; and A. T. Robertson, *Epochs in the Life of Jesus* (New York: Charles Scribner's Sons, 1921), pp. 98–119.

4. A. B. Bruce, *The Training of the Twelve*, 3d ed. (New York: Richard R. Smith, Inc., 1930).

5. Henry Latham, *Pastor Pastorum* (Cambridge: Deighton Bell and Co., 1910).

6. One almost hesitates to make a listing of these works since the degree of their significance to the thesis is so variable, and subject to interpretation, but at least the following selections that have come to my attention should be mentioned: Edwin A. Schell, *Traits of the Twelve* (Cincinnati: Jennings and Graham, 1911); Carl A. Glover, *With the Twelve* (Nashville: Cokesbury Press, 1939); F. Noel Palmer, *Christ's Way With People* (London: Marshall, Morgan & Scott, Ltd., 1943); and T. Ralph Morton, *The Twelve Together* (Glasgow: The Iona Community, 1956). Selected pages in other published works, to mention a few, are the chapters dealing with this subject in Alexander C. Purdy, *Jesus' Way With People* (New York: The Woman's Press, 1926), pp 101–15; and Alexander Rattray Hay, *The New Testament Order for*

Church and Missionary (Audubon, N.J.: New Testament Missionary Union, 1947), pp. 36–43. For an excellent updated bibliography in the whole area of discipleship, listing both scholarly and popular readings, consult the list prepared by Michael J. Wilkins in *Following the Master: Discipleship in the Steps of Jesus* (Grand Rapids: Zondervan, 1992), pp. 361–384.

Chapter 1—Selection

1. One qualification of an apostle mentioned in Acts 1:21, 22 was that he should have been with Jesus, "beginning from the baptism of John, unto the day that he was received up." Although this does not tell us from what point in John's baptismal work we are to begin (certainly not at the beginning or from the Lord's own baptism), it does argue for an early association of all the apostles with Jesus, perhaps dating from the time of John the Baptist's imprisonment. See Samuel J. Andrews, *op. cit.*, p. 268; cf., Alfred Edersheim, *op. cit.*, I. p. 521.

2. Many authors have sought to give us a picture of the twelve apostles. Among those which treat them all, in addition to those already cited in earlier footnotes, the following provide popular reading: George Matheson, *The Representative Men of the New Testament* (New York: Eaton & Mains, 1905); Edward Augustus George, *The Twelve* (New York: Fleming H. Revell, 1916); W. Mackintosh Mackay, *The Men Whom Jesus Made* (New York: George H. Doran Co., 1924); J. W. G. Ward, *The Master and the Twelve* (New York: George H. Doran Co., 1924); Charles R. Brown, *The Twelve* (New York: Harper, 1926); Francis Witherspoon, *The Glorious Company* (New York: Harcourt, Brace and Co., 1928); Asbury Smith, *The Twelve Christ Chose* (New York: Harper, 1958); William Barclay, *The Master's Men* (London: SCM Press, 1959); William Sanford LaSor, *Great Personalities of the New Testament* (Westwood, N.J.: Fleming H. Revell, 1961); J. Stuart Holden (London: Marshall, Morgan & Scott, 1953); and Ronald Brownrigg, *The Twelve Apostles* (New York: Macmillan, 1974).

3. Various opinions have been advanced as to why arbitrarily twelve disciples were designated apostles, for he could have selected more or gotten along with less, but probably the most plausible theory is that the number suggests a spiritual relationship of the apostolic company with the Messianic Kingdom of God. As Edwin Schell put it: "Twelve

is the number of the spiritual Israel. Whether observed in the twelve patriarchs, in the twelve tribes, or in the twelve foundations of the twelve gates of the heavenly Jerusalem, the number twelve everywhere symbolizes the indwelling of God in the human family—the interpenetration of the world by divinity," Schell, *op. cit.*, p. 26; cf., Bruce, *op. cit.*, p. 32. It is altogether possible that the apostles saw in the number a more literal meaning, and built up around it at first delusive hopes of the restoration of Israel in a political sense. They certainly were aware of their own place within the twelve, and were careful to fill up the vacancy created at the loss of Judas (Acts 1:15–26; cf., Matt. 19:28). One thing is certain, however, the number served to impress on those chosen their importance in the future work of the Kingdom.

4. Henry Latham suggests that the selection of these three served to impress on the whole company the need for "self-abnegation." In his analysis it actually was intended to show the apostles that "Christ gave what charge He would to whom He would; that in God's service it is honor enough to be employed at all; and that no man is to be discouraged because he sees allotted to another what appears to be a higher sphere of work than his own" Latham, *op. cit.*, p. 325.

5. The principle of concentration exemplified in the ministry of Jesus was not new with him. It had always been God's strategy from the beginning. The Old Testament records how God selected a comparatively small nation of Israel through which to effect his redemptive purpose for mankind. Even within the nation, the leadership was concentrated usually within family lines, especially the Davidic branch of the tribe of Judah.

6. The highpriestly prayer of Christ in the seventeenth chapter of John is especially meaningful in this connection. Of the twenty-six verses in the prayer, fourteen relate immediately to the twelve disciples (John 17:6–19).

7. This is not intended to suggest that this was all that was involved in the temptation, but only to emphasize that the temptation appealed to the strategy of Jesus for world evangelism as well as to the spiritual purpose of his mission. Another interpretation of this temptation experience from the standpoint of evangelistic method, somewhat similar, is given by Colin W. Williams in his book, *Where in the World?* (New York: National Council of Churches of Christ), pp. 24–27.

8. Instances of this are the case of the cleansed leper (Mark 1:44, 45; Matt. 8:4; Luke 5:14–16); those freed from unclean spirits by the Sea of Galilee (Mark 3:11, 12); Jairus after seeing his daughter raised from the dead (Mark 5:42, 43; Luke 8:55, 56); the two blind men restored to sight (Matt. 9:30); and the blind man in Bethsaida (Mark 8:25, 26).

9. Some examples of this are in John 1:29–43; 6:14, 15; Mark 4:35, 36; 6:1, 45, 46; 7:24–8:30; Matt. 8:18, 23; 14:22, 23; 15:21, 39; 16:4; Luke 5:16; 8:22; and others.

10. Examples of this are John 2:23–25; 6:30–60; 7:31–44; 11:45, 46; 12:11, 17–19; Luke 14:25–35; 19:36–38; Matt. 21:8–11, 14–17; Mark 11:8–11.

11. The Pharisees and Sadducees were the principal leaders of Israel, outside of the ruling Roman forces, and the whole religious, social, educational, and to a limited degree, political life of the approximately 2,000,000 people in Palestine was molded by their action. Yet the number of persons belonging to the Pharisaic guild, composed mostly of rabbis and well-to-do lay folk, according to the estimate of Josephus (*Ant.*, XVII, 2, 4), did not exceed 6,000; while the total number of Sadducees, made up mostly of the chief priests and Sanhedrin families in Jerusalem, probably did not amount to more than a few hundred. See Anthony C. Deane, *The World Christ Knew* (London: Guild Books, 1944), pp. 57, 60; Edersheim, *op. cit.*, I, p. 311. When it is considered that this small privileged group of less than 7,000 people, representing about one-third of one percent of the population of Israel, guided the spiritual destiny of a nation, it is not difficult to see why Jesus spoke so much about them, while also teaching his disciples the strategic need for better leadership.

12. This idea is brought out clearly in the translation of Ephesians 4:11 and 12 in the *New English Bible*, which reads: "And these were His gifts: some to be apostles, some prophets, some evangelists, some pastors and teachers, to equip God's people for work in His service, to the building up of the body of Christ." Other modern versions bring out the same essential meaning, including the Weymouth, Phillips, Wuest, Berkeley, Williams, and the Amplified New Testament. The three clauses in verse 12 are made successively dependent on the other, with the last being the climax. According to this interpretation, Christ gave a special gift to some officials in the church for the purpose of

perfecting the saints to do the service they have each to perform in the one great goal of building up Christ's body. The ministry of the church is seen as a work involving all members of the body (compare 1 Cor. 12:18 and 2 Cor. 9:8). Luther brings out the same thing in his commentary on "Ephesians," as also does Weiss, Meier, DeWitte, and Salmond. For a good exposition of this verse from this point of view, see the volume on Ephesians in *The Expositor's Greek Testament* (Grand Rapids: Wm. B. Eerdmans Publishing Co.), pp. 330–31. Other views are ably presented by Abbott in "Ephesians and Colossians," *International Critical Commentary* (Edinburgh: T. T. Clark, 1897), pp. 119, 120; and Lange, "Galatians–Colossians," *Commentary on the Holy Scriptures* (Grand Rapids: Zondervan), pp. 150–51. A practical treatment of this overall idea may be found in Gaines S. Dobbins's book, *A Ministering Church* (Nashville: Broadman Press, 1960), Ch. II, "A Church Needs Many Ministers," pp. 15–29; and from still another angle in Watchman Nee, *Normal Christian Church Life* (Washington, D.C.: International Students Press, 1962).

13. The collapse of communism at the end of the twentieth century is not due to its strategy, but to its moral and spiritual bankruptcy. Human beings cannot accept permanently a way of life that denigrates their personhood in the image of God.

14. For insight into the training program of the communist movement, see Douglas Hyde, *Dedication and Leadership* (South Bend: University of Notre Dame Press, 1966).

15. The number of adherents to Christianity has grown steadily across the years, but not as much as the non-Christian population. However, the picture is not as discouraging as it may appear. While the number of unevangelized people in the world has grown, the percentage of Christians compared to the total population continues to increase. From a positive point of view, then, the church should take heart, and with a greater sense of urgency and determination, complete the Great Commission mandate. A historical résumé of Christian numerical growth in reference to the world population as well as other religions can be found in the *World Christian Encyclopedia*, ed. by David B. Barrett (Oxford: Oxford University Press, 1982), pp. 3–19. For an insightful analysis of statistical patterns of growth, see the article by Ralph Winter, "When Feelings Bend Statistics," *International Journal of Frontier Missions*, 1991; or his update, "Are We

Losing the Battle? How to Kill Vision with Statistics," *Missions Frontiers*, May–June, 1992, 14:5–6, pp. 40–44.

Chapter 2—Association

1. Some scholars, like Henry Latham, have contended that prior to ordination of the apostles Jesus' first concern was with the multitudes, while afterward the emphasis shifted to the disciples, and especially to the Twelve (Henry Latham, *op. cit.*, pp. 188–269).Whether such a decisive division of concern is justified from the record or not, the fact is clear that Jesus did increasingly give himself to the apostolic company as time went on.

2. This fact was impressively recognized by the disciples, as Peter said: "Him God raised up the third day, and gave Him to be made manifest, not to all the people, but unto witnesses that were chosen before of God, even to us who did eat and drink with Him after He rose from the dead" (Acts 10:40, 41).

3. One cannot help but observe in this connection that the references to "the disciples" as a corporate body are much more frequent in the Gospels than are references to an individual disciple. T. Ralph Morton even goes further with this analogy and contends that most of the references to individuals refer to failures on their part, while the references to the group as a whole more often speak of their joy, understanding, or achievement. When it is remembered that these accounts were written under inspiration by the disciples, and not Jesus, it is quite significant that they would set forth their own place in such terms. See T. Ralph Morton, *op. cit.*, pp. 24–30, 103. We need not infer from this that the disciples were unimportant as individuals, for such was not the case, but it does impress us with the fact that the disciples understood their Lord to look on them as a body of believers being trained together for a common mission. They saw themselves through Christ first as a church, and secondly as individuals within that body.

Chapter 3—Consecration

1. At least sixteen times prior to his actual arrest by the soldiers Jesus spoke of his suffering and death. His first references were veiled with mystery, but the implication was clear—the comparison of his body to

the destruction of the temple (John 2:19); the reference to the Son of Man being lifted up like the brazen serpent (John 3:14); a remark concerning the day in which he as the bridegroom would be taken away (Mark 2:20; Matt. 9:15; Luke 5:35); the analogy of himself with the bread of life which had to be broken and eaten (John 6:51–58); and possibly the reference to the prophet Jonah as a sign (Matt. 16:4). Following the bold affirmation of Peter at Caesarea Philippi, Jesus began to show unto his disciples more boldly "how that he must go unto Jerusalem, and suffer many things, and be rejected by the elders, and chief priests, and the scribes, and be killed, and after three days rise again" (Mark 8:31; Matt. 16:21; Luke 9:22). Thereafter he foretold his death and resurrection with detail while passing through Galilee with his disciples (Mark 9:30–32; Matt. 17:22, 23; Luke 9:43–45); and again on his last journey to Jerusalem after his ministry in Perea (Mark 10:33, 34; Matt. 20:18–19; Luke 18:32–33). His decease was the subject of his conversation with Moses and Elijah on the Mount of Transfiguration (Luke 9:31). It was also implied by his remark about a prophet not perishing out of Jerusalem (Luke 13:33), as well as the reference to the suffering and rejection of the people before his return in glory (Luke 17:25). He likened himself to a Good Shepherd "who layeth down his life for the sheep" (John 10:11, 18), and as a grain of wheat that falls to the earth and dies before it could bring forth fruit (John 12:24). A few days before the last Passover Jesus again reminded his disciples that he would be "delivered up to be crucified" (Matt. 26:2), and later the same day he explained in the house of Simon the leper that the precious ointment which Mary poured over his feet was in preparation for his burial (Mark 14:8; Matt. 26:12). Finally, at his last supper with his disciples Jesus told of his impending suffering (Luke 22:15), and then initiated the memorial of his death by eating bread and drinking wine (Mark 14:22–25; Matt. 26:26–29; Luke 22:17–20).

Chapter 4—Impartation

1. Sanctification is used also in reference to Jesus in John 10:36, where again the idea is basically evangelistic in application.

2. The tenses of the word *sanctify* reveal one important difference between the sanctification of Jesus and that of his disciples. The word for the Master's sanctification is in the present indicative, indicating a

continuous condition—"I continue to sanctify myself." On the other hand, when Jesus refers to his disciples in the next phrase, the perfect passive participle is used with the words "to be," making a paraphrastic construction which means here that there is a definite crisis of commitment in the sanctification of the disciples, though the emphasis is still largely on the continuing result of that crisis. An expanded free interpretation of this passage in John 17:19 might read thus: "For their sakes I continually—moment by moment—renew my commitment to the work of evangelism, and I am willing to make every sacrifice necessary to accomplish this purpose of God for my life. And because I know that nothing else will suffice if the work of God is to be carried on in the future, I am asking the same of you. I have appointed you to go out and do my work, but before you will really feel my compassion for the lost world, you will have to make a full commitment of all that you are and all that you have to God's plan of world evangelism, and keep it up every day of your lives." I believe that such a dedication taken to heart would do more for the evangelization of the world than anything else. Surely it is a dimension of the sanctified life that needs more emphasis.

3. This verse in John 14:12 has an application to evangelism that is staggering to comprehend, for not only does it say that all believers "will do the works of Christ," but it also says that they will do "greater works" because Jesus was going to the Father. Taken as it stands, this passage would teach us that the disciples as a body in the power of the Holy Spirit were to do everything which their Lord had done—and that takes in quite a bit—and yet do even more. As to what these greater deeds were to be, Jesus did not say, but from the Acts of the Apostles it would obviously be in the realm of evangelism. At least, in this respect, the church actually did see more results than Christ. In fact, just in one day at Pentecost more people were added to the church than had been accumulated during the three years of Jesus' ministry.

4. The word *another* here is of a peculiar significance in the original Greek. It is not the word used to compare two objects of a dissimilar quality, but rather the word used to compare two things of the same essential quality, there being a difference only in person. Hence the value of this word is that it identifies the quality of the Spirit with that of the incarnate Son, so that the Spirit, while different in person, is exactly like Jesus in his ministry to the disciples. See G. Campbell Mor-

gan, *The Teaching of Christ* (New York: Revell, 1913), p. 65. Excellent treatment of Jesus' teaching about the Spirit's work may be found in Louis Burton Crane, *The Teaching of Jesus Concerning the Holy Spirit* (New York: American Tract Society, 1905); And J. Ritchie Smith, *The Holy Spirit in the Gospels* (New York: Macmillan, 1926).

5. This promise was fulfilled to the disciples at Pentecost (Acts 2:4). However, it did not end there. Repeatedly Luke calls to our attention that the infilling of the Holy Spirit was the abiding and sustaining experience of the early church (Acts 4:8, 31; 6:3, 5; 7:55; 9:17; 11:24; 13:9, 52). Certainly from this it would appear that the Spirit-filled life was accepted as the norm of Christian experience, although it was not a reality to all. This is why, for example, Paul was constrained to exhort the Ephesians to "be filled with the Holy Spirit" (Eph. 5:18). In this connection, it would be good to read William Arthur, *The Tongue of Fire* (London: The Epworth Press, 1956); John Wesley, *A Plain Account of Christian Perfection* (London: Epworth Press, n.d.); Samuel Chadwick, *The Way to Pentecost* (New York: Fleming H. Revell, 1932); Charles G. Finney, "Be Filled with the Spirit," in *Revival Lectures* (New York: Fleming H. Revell, 1958); Andrew Murray, *The Full Blessing of Pentecost* (London: Oliphants Ltd., 1954); Samuel Logan Brengle, *When the Holy Ghost Is Come* (New York: Salvation Army Printing and Publishing House, 1911); R. A. Torrey, *The Baptism With the Holy Spirit* (New York: Fleming H. Revell, 1895); V. R. Edman, *They Found the Secret* (Grand Rapids: Zondervan, 1960); and the sermon "How to be Filled with the Holy Spirit" by Billy Graham, *Revival in Our Time* (Wheaton, Ill.: VanKampen, 1950), just to mention a few of the more popular presentations of this subject. Terminology used in describing this experience may vary depending on one's particular theological perspective, but a study of Christian history will reveal that the reality of the experience itself, howsoever it may be defined, is common to those who have been greatly used of God in making the gospel relevant to others.

6. A good example of this is the famous Sermon on the Mount (Matt. 5:3–7:27; Luke 6:20–49). It was not addressed primarily to the wayfaring crowd, although they overheard it (Matt. 7:28, 29). Rather this sublime statement concerning the moral and ethical conduct of the Kingdom was delivered to those few close followers who could appreciate it. "Seeing this multitude, he went up into the mountain;

and when he was set down, his disciples came unto him, and he opened his mouth and taught them" (Matt. 5:1, 2; cf., Luke 6:17–20). Perhaps the most striking illustration of the deliberate way that Jesus withheld teaching from those who did not want it is the way he guarded his own association with the messianic promise. Although he made this claim to his friends early in his ministry (John 4:25, 26, 42), and allowed his disciples to affirm it from the beginning (John 1:41, 45, 49), there is no record that he ever declared that he was the Messiah to the religious rulers of Jerusalem until he was on trial, and then only after the high priest asked him point-blank if he was the Christ (Mark 14:61, 62; Matt. 26:63, 64).

Chapter 5—Demonstration

1. More than twenty times the Gospels call attention to Jesus' practice of prayer. It is given special mention during events of momentous decision in his life—baptism (Luke 3:21); the selection of the twelve apostles (Luke 6:12); on the Mount of Transfiguration (Luke 9:29); the Last Supper (Matt. 26:27); in Gethsemane (Luke 22:39–46); and on the cross (Luke 23:46). The Revelators also were impressed to record their Lord's intercession in connection with their own ministry—the confession of his messiahship (Luke 9:18); on hearing their reports of evangelism (Luke 10:21, 22); teaching them to pray (Luke 11:1); the great highpriestly prayer before he goes to die (John 17:6–19); the loving concern for Peter (Luke 22:32); and at the home of the two disciples in Emmaus after the resurrection (Luke 24:30). Prayer is prominent also in the exercise of his power-working miracles—healing the multitudes (Mark 1:35); feeding the five thousand (Mark 6:41; Matt. 14:19; Luke 9:16; John 6:11); later feeding the four thousand (Mark 8:6; Matt. 15:36); healing the deaf-mute (Mark 7:34); and raising Lazarus from the dead (John 11:41). Moreover, prayer is on the lips of Jesus as he looks at the multitudes whom he came to save—before conflict with religious leaders (Luke 5:16); in the discussion with the Greeks who came to see him (John 12:27); after sending away the five thousand who had been fed (Mark 6:46; Matt. 14:23); blessing little children (Mark 10:16); and finally for those who nailed him to the cross (Luke 23:34).

2. There was never any confusion in his mind respecting their cred-
ibility and witness, for he knew that they were inspired by the Holy
Spirit (Mark 12:36; Matt. 22:43). The written Scriptures were for him
"the Word of God" (John 10:35; Mark 7:13; Matt. 15:6; cf., Luke
8:12). Indeed, in a unique sense, they were his own Word which he
interpreted and deepened (e.g., Matt. 5:21, 22, 27, 28), as he declared,
"These are they which bear witness of Me" (John 5:39; cf., Matt. 5:17,
18). In this consciousness, he full well realized that his life was the fulfillment of Scripture, and frequently he called attention to that fact
(Matt. 5:18; 8:17; 13:14; 26:54, 56; Mark 14:49; Luke 4:21; 21:22;
John 13:18; 15:25; 17:12). It is only natural, then, that Jesus utilized
this ready source of sure knowledge in his work. This was the food
which nourished his soul (Matt. 4:4) and fortified his heart against
temptation (Matt. 4:4, 7, 10; 12:3; Luke 4:4, 8, 12). But above all, it
was his textbook for teaching in public and private the eternal truth
of God (e.g., Luke 4:17–21; 24:27, 32, 44, 45).

3. These are separate instances of his spoken word in which some
reference is made to the Old Testament, either by direct quotation,
allusion to some event, or language similar to words used in Jewish
Scriptures. Counting duplications in parallel accounts of the same event
there are altogether about 160 references in the four Gospels where
Jesus alludes to the Bible of his day. Furthermore, two-thirds of the
Old Testament books are included in these references. In view of this,
one can conclude that the word of Christ was thoroughly imbued with
the teaching of the old patriarchs, kings, and prophets. His whole
thought was cast in the spirit of the inspired writings of his day. See
Herman Harrell Horne, *Jesus the Master Teacher* (New York: Association Press, 1920), pp. 93–106; and J. M. Price, *op. cit.*, 8–11, 62–64.
Virtually a complete list of these various Old Testament references in
the Gospels may be found in A. T. Robertson, *Harmony of the Gospels
for Students of the Life of Christ* (New York: Harper & Brothers, 1922),
pp. 295–301.

4. The limits of this discussion do not permit an exhaustive treatment of all the practices of Jesus which affected his life. His manner
in regard to teaching the disciples to pray and use the Bible is mentioned only as an example of how careful he was to prepare his followers for service. To adequately cover the subject, one must consider
his practice of worship, his concern for the rituals and laws of society,

his attitude in regard to civil and social responsibilities, just to mention a few. But the point is that in all these things Jesus taught his disciples how to live a relevant and victorious life in the midst of a pagan world. For further comments and resources pertaining to the inner disciplines of Christ, see my book, *The Mind of Christ* (Revell, 1977).

5. Numerous authors have sought to analyze the teaching techniques of Jesus, and the student who wants to pursue this subject further would do well to consult some of these works, such as, D. M. Ross, *The Teaching of Jesus* (Edinburgh: T. & T. Clark, 1904), esp. pp. 46–59; George Barker Stevens, *The Teaching of Jesus* (New York: Macmillan, 1918), pp. 33–46; Charles Francis McKay, *The Art of Jesus as a Teacher* (Philadelphia: The Judson Press, 1930); and Luther Allan Weigle, *Jesus and the Educational Method* (New York: Abingdon, 1939). Works by Horne, Squires, Richardson, and Price, mentioned in an earlier footnote, also provide very helpful insights.

6. Other instances of this same thing follow the parable of the tares (Matt. 13:36f.); his rebuke to the Pharisees for making void the Word of God by their traditions (Matt. 15:15f.); the lesson on the rich young fool (Luke 12:22f.); the parable of the rich man and Lazarus (Luke 17:1f.); his word to the Pharisees concerning the coming of the kingdom (Luke 17:22f.); and the matter of divorce according to the law of Moses (Mark 10:10f.; Matt. 19:7f.).

Chapter 6—Delegation

1. I cannot restrain the observation here that the disciples of Jesus were given the privilege of administering the rite of baptism considerably before they were ordained to preach. If we were to deduce from this a rule of ecclesiastical policy, it would imply certainly that the preaching ministry is more significant and wrought with more dangers and privileges than a ministry of the sacraments, at least, of baptism. Anyone thus entrusted with the sacred ministry of the Word has a much more responsible position than merely administering baptism, and thus the greater responsibility should include the lesser. The application of this policy, however, would have some far-reaching ramifications in many communions of the modern church.

2. The plan of going out in pairs seemed to be a practice followed often in the Gospels. For example, two disciples were sent to find the

colt for Jesus to use in entering Jerusalem (Luke 19:29). Peter and John together are sent to make ready the Passover (Luke 22:8). It is probable that James and John were together on their mission before Jesus into Samaria since they are the ones loud in indignation at their reception (Luke 9:52, 54). James T. Vance in his little volume, *The College of Apostles* (New York: Fleming H. Revell, 1896), even attempts to view all the apostles in terms of pairs, making altogether six groups of two within the company. His idea is that the disciples were matched up to complement the other's virtues and to minimize the other's faults. His grouping put together Peter the extremist with Andrew the conservative; James the elder with John the youth; Philip the dullard with Bartholomew the sage; Thomas the man of doubts with Matthew the man of strong conviction; James the champion of duty with Jude the champion of doctrine; and Simon the Zealot with Judas the traitor. The support for this supposition rests largely on the listing of the apostles in pairs by Matthew (Matt. 10:2–4). Latham, *op. cit.*, p. 162. In all fairness, I think that we must recognize that this grouping is mostly hypothetical. Nevertheless, it is a matter of record that the Book of Acts represents the apostles and missionaries of the Church traveling in groups of two or more.

Chapter 7—Supervision

1. Before Jesus fed the five thousand, he first asked the disciples to give the people something to eat. This was done purposely to show them their little faith (John 6:6), and also to impress on them the problem created thereby. It was only after the disciples were convinced of their utter helplessness in the face of this situation that Jesus intervened, yet even then he used the disciples in his solution to the problem.

2. It is significant that he was careful to teach them that the Holy Spirit would continue to supervise their work after he had turned them loose from his incarnate direction. The Christian worker never is without personal supervision.

Chapter 8—Reproduction

1. Lest someone misconstrue this optimism to suppose that the evangelization of the world stressed here negates the need or the fact

of Christ's glorious Second Coming, let me reiterate that the preaching of the gospel only prepares the way for the Lord's return (Matt. 24:14). It neither discounts the personal intervention of Christ at the end time nor implies that the Kingdom will come as a result of human ingenuity. This is true regardless of what particular millennial view one might hold.

2. The personal nature of the address is sometimes obscured by those who seek to avoid any suggestion that Peter was given supremacy in the church. Such concern is unnecessary for there is nothing in the passage, or anywhere else in the Bible, that lends credence to the Roman Catholic pretensions for the papacy. To say even that the "rock" refers to Peter, as many exegetes do, merely underscores his prominence and leadership in affirming the faith of Christ. See this view in A. B. Bruce, *The Expositor's Greek Testament*, ed. by Nicoll, Reprint (Grand Rapids: Eerdmans), pp. 224, 225; Philip Vollmer, *The Modern Life of Christ* (New York: Revell, 1912), pp. 162, 163; also the commentaries of Meyer, Alford, Brown, and Bengel. However, other scholars prefer to disassociate from Peter the "rock" upon which the Church is here said to be built. They follow several lines of interpretation, especially the idea that the "rock" means Peter's confession of faith. An example is A. T. Robertson, *Word Pictures in the New Testament*, I (New York, 1930), pp. 131–33; also the commentaries of Luther and Clark, as well as the *Pilgrim Bible*. Closely akin to this view, and often intermingled with it, is the opinion that the "rock" is Christ himself. For example, the notes in *Berkeley* and *Scofield* Bibles support this position as also do Augustine and Jerome. Others believe that it is applied to Peter as a representative of all believers. An example of this interpretation is John Calvin, *Commentary on a Harmony of the Evangelists*, II, Reprint (Grand Rapids, Eerdmans, 1949), p. 291. A number of these men make much of the fact that in the Greek text the word *Peter* (πέτρος) is in the masculine gender, while the word translated "rock" (πέτρα) is in the feminine. This distinction makes it possible from the use of the words elsewhere to see Peter as "a piece of rock formation" in contrast to the "rock formation itself" on which the church was to rest. However, regardless of one's view at this point, the fact still remains that Peter was spoken to personally by Christ, and he could not have been considered even as a piece of the rock had he not personally affirmed his faith in Christ's deity. This conclusion seems to me to stand as an obvi-

ous truth beyond any of the interpretations given to the "rock" cited above.

3. See Peter Lange for an interesting analysis of the way Peter's faithfulness of confession is regarded as the proper interpretation of the "rock," which amounts really to another point of view on this subject. Peter Lange, *Commentary on the Holy Scriptures*, Matthew, Reprint (Grand Rapids, Zondervan), p. 298. The view stated in my presentation here, however, relates to the whole temper of the passage, and not to any particular word.

4. It is noteworthy that Peter himself makes this analogy. Furthermore, the absence of any claim of personal superiority in his letters indicates convincingly that Peter did not understand his Lord as bestowing any special ecclesiastical or spiritual authority on him.

5. It is interesting, too, that in this whole passage, every time fruit-bearing is mentioned, the word is in the present tense, which means in the Greek text that it is a continuing thing—something that just keeps on reproducing.

6. I am indebted to Dr. Roland G. Leavell for first calling this to my attention in his book, *Evangelism, Christ's Imperative Commission* (Nashville: Broadman Press, 1951), p. 3. The participle "go," however, does stand in a coordinate relationship with the verb which makes it also an imperative. I was surprised to find that none of the commentaries which I checked in reference to this passage seemed to take note of the Greek grammar which justifies the emphasis of the participles cited above.

7. Dawson Trotman, *Born to Reproduce* (Lincoln, Nebr.: Back to the Bible Publishers, 1959), p. 42. This little booklet by the founder of the Navigators is something that every person interested in this subject should read.

8. An attempt to exegete these principles in the Book of Acts is in my book, *The Master Plan of Discipleship* (Revell, 1987).

9. E. M. Bounds, *Power Through Prayer*, Reprint (Grand Rapids: Baker Book House), p. 7. The account of every great revival and missionary movement in church history will prove the truth of this statement. That is why, outside of the Bible, reading Christian biography will do more to stimulate evangelism than anything else. It would be a good idea to follow a varied and regular plan of reading in this area. Numerous books are available, but among them one should read by

all means the *Life and Diary of David Brainerd*, edited by Jonathan Edwards (Chicago: Moody Press, 1949); Dr. and Mrs. Howard Taylor's account of their father in *Hudson Taylor's Spiritual Secret* (London: China Inland Mission, 1950); the *Memoirs of Rev. Charles G. Finney* (New York: Fleming H. Revell Co., 1873); Clarence Wilbur Hall's story of the saintly Brengel, *Portrait of a Prophet* (New York: Salvation Army, 1933); and Jim Elliot's discipline of life compiled from his letters and diary by his wife, Elisabeth Elliot in *Under the Shadow of the Almighty* (New York: Harper & Brothers, 1958). These and other similar true stories of men with vision and dedication will challenge us to do more for God.

Epilogue—The Master and Your Plan

1. In the past thirty years a number of significant books on discipleship have been published, including works by Allan Coppedge, Matt Friedman, Bill Hull, Keith Phillips, Walter Henrichsen, Carl Wilson, William A. Shell, Leroy Eims, Christopher Adsit, Myron Augsburger, Howard Belben, Michael Wilkins, Francis Cosgrove, David Dawson, Ajith Fernando, Leighton Ford, Doug Hartman, Ernest Best, Ron Kincaid, Gary Kuhne, Carole Mayhall, Dwight Pentecost, Allan Hadidian, Fernando Segovia, Scott McKnight, and D. Stuart Briscoe. This list of authors, though by no means complete, indicates the growing interest in this subject. Increasing concern is also reflected in the proliferation of discipleship programs available from various denominational and para-church publishing houses. Students should avail themselves of these resources.

2. There is no want of information relative to the function and operation of small groups. Various aspects of the concept are treated in books by Samuel Shoemaker, Elton Trueblood, Harry C. Munro, Harold Freer, Francis B. Hall, John Casteel, Paul Miller, Richard Peace, Steve Barker, Ron Nicholas, Howard Snyder, David Prior, Jimmy Long, Judy Johnson, Lawrence O. Richards, Dennis Benson, Dan Williams, Judy Hamlin, Jeffrey Arnold, Em Griffin, Neal F. McBride, Carl George, Howard Ball, Ralph Neighbor, Paul Y. Cho, and a host of others. To this literature can be added a whole range of group study and discussion guides that can be found in almost any Christian bookstore. If you want to see how groups can excite people, get into the

materials prepared by Lyman Coleman, published by Serendipity, P.O. Box 1012, Littleton, CO 80160. An excellent overview of his approach is the *Serendipity Bible for Groups* (1989).

3. Adapted from Billy Graham, "Billy Graham Speaks: The Evangelical World Prospect," and exclusive interview in *Christianity Today*, Vol. III, No. 1, October 13, 1958, p. 5. Used by permission.

4. Much has been said about the recovery of the lay ministry, but no book puts the issue any better than that of Paul Rees, *Stir Up the Gift* (Grand Rapids: Zondervan, 1952). Other forthright applications of this idea can be found in J. E. Conant, *Every Member Evangelism* (New York: Harper & Brothers, 1922); Tom Allan, *The Face of My Parish* (New York: Harper & Brothers, 1953); Elton Trueblood, *The Company of the Committed* (New York: Harper & Brothers, 1961); and the thrilling missionary story of *Evangelism-in-Depth* (Chicago: Moody Press, 1961). A related work, written from the standpoint of missions, which has had a great impact since it first appeared a generation ago is the book by Roland Allen, *Missionary Methods: St. Paul's or Ours* (London: World Dominion Press, 1953), and its companion volume, *The Spontaneous Expansion of the Church* (London: World Dominion Press, 1949).

5. The materials dealing with methods of personal evangelism are plentiful and generally accessible. Since there are so many different ways to approach the subject, it would be well to peruse several different authors who have written in the field, among them James Kennedy, S. L. Brengel, F. D. Whitesell, Joseph Aldrich, L. R. Scarborough, Bill Bright, Horace F. Dean, Leroy Eims, William Evans, Tom L. Eisenman, Ann Kiemel, Gene Edwards, Leighton Ford, E. M. Harrison, Billy Hanks, Jr., Nate Krupp, Howard Hendricks, Paul Little, Lorne C. Sanny, R. A. Torrey, Walton L. Wilson, Beth Mainhood, J. O. Sanders, Mark McCloskey, G. Campbell Morgan, Stephen Olford, Jim Peterson, S. A. Witmer, Donald Paterski, Charles Kingsley, Matthew Prince, William G. Schweer, Charles Shaver, John R. W. Stott, Stanley Tom, Jill Briscoe, Oscar Thompson, Charles Trumbull, Robert Tuttle, Jack Voelkel, and H. Clay Trumbull, to mention a few. A simple introduction to this subject might be the representative selection of twelve Gospel communicators compiled by Joel D. Heck, *The Art of Sharing Your Faith* (Tarrytown: Fleming H. Revell, 1991).

6. Follow-up is the first step in discipleship. Persons wanting more direction in this particular ministry will find helpful the writings of Charlie Riggs, David Dawson, Gene and Erma Warr, Lorne Sanny, Hal Brooks, Arthur C. Archibald, Winkie Pratney, Frances M. Cosgrove, Roy Robertson, Gary Kuhne, Roy Fish, Charles Shaver, and Billy Hanks, Jr. As an introduction, see Waylon B. Moore's *New Testament Follow-Up for Pastors and Laymen* (Grand Rapids: Wm. B. Eerdmans, 1972).

7. As in the case of personal work, there continues to be a great deal written in the practical field of church evangelism and the related area of church growth. Among the many resources are books by Leith Anderson, George Sweagey, Charles and Win Arn, C. E. Autrey, Andrew Blackwood, John Bisagno, William B. Riley, J. E. Conant, Roy Fish, Elmer Towns, Michael Green, Sterling Huston, Ralph Neighbor, Bailey Smith, Paul Y. Cho, George Hunter, Donald McGavran, Charles Shumate, Roy H. Short, Bernard and Marjorie Palmer, Myron Augsburger, John S. Starn, Louis Drummond, Mendal Taylor, Peter Wagner, Carl George, John Wimber, Jack Hyles, Charles L. Goodell, George Barna, James Engel, Kent Hunter, Larry Lewis, Greg Ogden, Calvin Ratz, Roland G. Leavell, W. E. Sangster, and Samuel A. Shoemaker. Most denominational publishing houses also have materials designed to help churches develop programs of evangelism.

Study guide for
The Master Plan of Evangelism

Roy J. Fish

Introduction

One of the critical issues facing evangelical Christians in today's world has to do with an overall strategy of evangelism. The basic objective of this *study guide* is to assist you in discovering the evangelistic strategy of Jesus as set forth in the New Testament and as interpreted in the book, *The Master Plan of Evangelism* by Robert E. Coleman. The central goals of the *study guide* are as follows:

1. To encourage exploration of the Gospels in search of Jesus' strategy.
2. To review the meaning and values of the principles set forth by him.
3. To lead to a deeper commitment to his plan.
4. To lead to an implementation of his strategy in our lives.

As to how the *study guide* can be most effectively used, two suggestions might be of help. First it is designed for you to write in, so study it with a pencil in hand. Second, have a New Testament near for handy reference.

The guide is composed of thirteen lessons. Each lesson will be similar in outline. First, there is a brief summary of the content of the chapter or particular section of *The Master Plan* which is to be studied. This section sets forth the central idea or main thrust of the chapter and calls attention

139

to basic learning goals for the chapter. Following is a section, Learning Procedures, containing questions which are designed to lead one to search out the major contents of a chapter. Only one chapter at a time should be done and, if possible, enough time set aside for the completion of the lesson at one sitting. Answers to questions, where needed, will be found at the end of the guide.

This section is followed by suggestions for group discussion and group activities. As groups study the guide, it will be helpful if each member answers the questions in the Learning Procedures before the group meets.

The ultimate objective of the study is the implementation of the master plan in the life of the reader. For this reason, each lesson will suggest some achievement goals and procedures which encourage personal application of the strategy of Jesus. Concluding each chapter is a brief section which offers ideas for further research of material appropriate for that chapter. A complete bibliography is given in the back of the book.

This *study guide* is sent forth with the prayer that your life will be richly blessed by it and that it will be of assistance to you in discovering and implementing the plan of the Master for your own life.

Roy J. Fish

Note: Some of the materials recommended when this guide was first published may no longer be available.

Lesson 1
The Master and His Plan

There seems to be renewed interest in the church today toward obeying the Great Commission of our Lord. Accompanying this concern, a great deal of thought is being given to new and creative methods of evangelism. But along with quickened interest and creativity in methods, there comes an imperative regarding another matter which is even more vital. This imperative has to do with strategy, and more particularly with restudying the basic evangelistic strategy of Jesus himself.

That Jesus moved on earth with a deliberate strategy of evangelism is a fact about which there can be little question. He kept clearly before him the fact that he had come "to seek and to save that which was lost" (Luke 19:10). He ordered his life by this objective. All Jesus ever said or did was a part of the divine strategy of evangelism for him. But the concept the church of today must never overlook is that *as he was executing his plan, he was also setting forth a strategy of evangelism for his church for all time.*

Consequently, it is not the task of the church to invent a *new* strategy. Our task is to *rediscover* his and to get in step with it. There is abundant evidence that the following of past traditions and the conformity to present religious culture have kept many churches from capturing his concept of strategy. When we do catch sight of it, it proves to be so different that its implications are nothing short of revolutionary. But for his best blessings to be on our efforts in evangelism, we must approximate the plan of the Master as nearly as possible. It must be done, even at the price of jettisoning some unnecessary religious activities and of altering some sacred organizational structures.

Learning Procedures

1. For approximately sixty seconds, look at the table of contents of *The Master Plan of Evangelism*. Listed below are the chapter headings in mixed order. After you have studied the proper order, see if you can arrange them correctly. Check the table of contents and compare your order with it.
   Supervision _____
   Delegation _____
   Selection _____
   Association _____
   Consecration _____
   Reproduction _____
   Impartation _____
   Demonstration _____

2. On page 19, the author speaks of "the evangelistic activity of the church." Write below your definition of evangelism.

3. When Dr. Coleman employs the word *strategy*, which of the three words below is most similar to what he means? Put a check after it.
   Objectives _____
   Methods _____
   Principles _____

4. The best textbook on evangelism in print is _____.
5. Answer the following true-or-false questions by writing T or F in the blank space which corresponds to the question.
   a. Jesus made a clear distinction between home and foreign missions. _____
   b. The eight steps of guiding principles of Jesus to train men come invariably in a deliberately planned sequence. _____
   c. Method and strategy in evangelism are essentially the same thing. _____

Group Discussion and Activity

Group discussion will center around four closely related questions. They should be discussed in the order in which they are found here.

1. Discuss the primary objective for a church according to Jesus. Look at the Great Commissions found in Matthew 28:19, John 20:21, and Acts 1:8.
2. Take an objective look at your church or Christian group and compare the objectives of your church or group to his.
3. Then ask: Is the organization and activity of our church or group really set up to achieve the basic objectives of Jesus?
4. What changes could be made so that your church or group will more nearly approximate the objectives of our Lord?

Achievement Goals

At the outset of this study, test yourself as to past achievement in evangelism:

1. I tell other people about Christ with a view to win them to him
   frequently _____
   sometimes _____
   seldom _____
   never _____

2. I attempt to assist believers in becoming more mature in their Christian lives
   frequently _____
   sometimes _____
   seldom _____
   never _____

3. Ask yourself: Do I have a strategy of evangelism for my own life? If not, am I willing to become a part of his?

Ideas for Further Research

1. A series of four cassette tapes by D. James Kennedy of Coral Ridge Presbyterian Church in Fort Lauderdale, Florida, are extremely helpful for this entire study. They are produced by David C. Cook Publishing Company, Elgin, Illinois. Tape #1 is particularly appropriate for this chapter.

2. The film, *Charlie Churchman and the Church Week,* Gospel Films, Muskegon, Michigan 49440, is a pointed caricature of busy Christians who are really doing nothing to fulfill the real mission of the church.

Lesson 2
Selection

In considering the Master's plan, one cannot help but be struck by its simplicity. It is best described by the phrase "concentration on a few." Its beginning was very unobtrusive as Jesus called a handful of men merely to follow him. One is hardly impressed with the outward qualifications of the small group. They were rather common, to say the least, but they were teachable. And it was on this small group that Jesus concentrated his earthly ministry.

It should not be thought for a minute that Jesus completely neglected the many for the purpose of ministry to the few. The vision of the multitudes was always before him and frequently the Gospel records make reference to his ministry to the masses. But Jesus was wise enough to see that before the multitudes could be permanently helped, they would need more personal care than he alone could give. His real hope of ministry to them lay in training a small group who could later lead the multitudes in the things of God.

The pattern of Jesus should teach us that the first duty of a spiritual leader is to lay a foundation on which an evangelistic ministry can be built. Laying such a foundation will require concentration of effort on the time and talents of a few. Though the obvious results of such a plan will likely be slower in coming and probably unnoticed by most, the amount of good done and the number of people reached will ultimately be far greater.

Learning Procedures

1. Of the three answers to each of the questions listed below, circle the one which is correct.
   a. Most of the disciples came from Galilee. The only one who seems to have come from Judea was: Thomas, Judas, Peter.
   b. The total number of devoted followers of Jesus at the time of his death was around: 100, 500, 10,000.
   c. Within the select apostolic group, three seemed to enjoy a more special relationship to the Master. One of them was: Andrew, Matthew, John.

2. Fill in the blank spaces of the sentences below with the correct words. Use the text to find them.
   a. Jesus' concern was not with _____ to reach the multitudes, but with _____ whom the multitudes would follow.
   b. The initial objective of Jesus' plan was _____ and after he returned to the Father.
   c. The men called by Jesus are described by the author as being _____, _____, _____, and having all the _____ of their environment.
   d. One cannot transform a _____ except as _____ in the world are _____, and _____ cannot be changed except as they are molded in the hands of the Master.

3. Answer the following true-or-false questions by writing T or F in the blank space in front of the question.

———— a. In giving so much time to the Twelve, Jesus demonstrated unconcern for the masses.

———— b. Jesus' call to the Twelve to follow him made immediate impact upon the religious life of his day.

———— c. The word which best describes the basic principles of Jesus in his ministry to those he intended to use is concentration.

Group Discussion and Activity

1. Look up the Scripture passage 2 Timothy 2:2. Discuss its similarity to the principle employed by Jesus. Draw a diagram to illustrate the principle.

Paul   Timothy   Faithful Men   Others

2. On page 34, Dr. Coleman states that, if one were to "measure the effectiveness of his evangelism by the number of converts, Jesus doubtless would not be considered among the most productive mass evangelists of the church." If this is true, in what sense can we consider Jesus a great evangelist? After discussion, read the section, "His Strategy," pages 34–36.

3. Discuss possible objections to the principle of concentration on the few.

4. Discuss the sentence, "In an age when facilities for rapid communication of the gospel are available to the church as never before, we are actually accomplishing less in winning the world for God than before the invention of the horseless carriage."

Achievement Goals

1. Make a list of possible opportunities of association which you might have with a new or immature Christian. Some will be readymade, i.e., a Sunday school teacher with a class; or if you are a deacon, elder, or steward, perhaps you are responsible for certain members. Other opportunities will need to be planned.
2. Ask God to lead you to at least one person with whom you can work and lead to a life of discipleship.
3. Determine what requirements you will look for in the person.
4. List some things you want to see accomplished in this person's life.

Ideas for Further Research

1. For further reading material related to this chapter, the following would be helpful. (See bibliography for complete information on suggested books.)
   a. Chapters one and two in the book, *Pastor Pastorum* by Henry Latham.
   b. Chapter one of the book, *The Men Whom Jesus Made* by W. Mackintosh Mackay.
   c. The chapter entitled, "Characteristics of His Pupils," in the book, *Jesus the Teacher* by J. M. Price.
   d. Part three of the book, *The Apostles of Our Lord* by J. G. Greenbough.

2. Tape #2 of the Kennedy cassettes, mentioned in Lesson One, deals with the manner in which a contemporary church selects people for ministry.

Lesson 3
Association

The essence of the training program of Jesus was simply having his disciples with him. To train men for world conquest he just drew them close to himself. They learned first by association with him. Jesus knew that in his presence his followers could learn what they really needed to know. It should be no surprise then that as the ministry of Jesus lengthened into its second and third years, he gave an increased amount of time to the Twelve. Almost everything Jesus is recorded as having done, he did in the presence of at least some of his disciples. *He was building men by being with them.*

The church today has been slow to come to grips with this principle. Efforts by mature Christians to follow up the maturing of believers have lacked the aspect of personal attention needed by immature Christians. As a result of slipshod methods of follow-up, about 50 percent of those who unite with local churches eventually become inactive. The attempt has been made to produce disciples on an assembly-line basis and the results have been disastrous. Some system must be found whereby every new Christian may be taken under the wing of a mature believer and encouraged to stay there until he or she has matured to the point of leading another. To train people for this follow-up ministry is a current imperative facing every church that does not already have such a program.

Learning Procedures

1. To illustrate the point of association of the disciples with Jesus, the eighth and ninth chapters of Luke show at least a dozen experiences where the disciples were with him. At least eight times they had opportunity to observe him as he worked. List them below.

_____   _____

_____   _____

_____   _____

_____   _____

2. Fill in the blank spaces with correct answers.
   a. The essence of the training program of Jesus was
      _____.
   b. Knowledge was gained by _____ before it was understood by _____.
   c. Three other illustrations of follow-up, over and above the Twelve, were _____, _____, and _____.

3. Circle the correct answer in the following questions.
   a. During the second and third years of his ministry, Jesus gave (more) (less) time to the Twelve.
   b. Approximately (1/5) (1/3) (1/2) of the people who join a local church ultimately fall away.
   c. All ten of the resurrection appearances of Jesus were to (unbelievers, that they might believe) (the disciples and Jewish leaders) (the disciples only).

Group Discussion and Activity

1. Secure the figure representing the total membership of your church or group. Then discuss the following:

a. How many of our members attend Bible study or Sunday school?

b. What percentage are faithful to the worship services?

c. How many attend prayer meetings?

d. How many are involved in some kind of Christian ministry?

e. If the small percentages impress you, discuss the question: Why so few?

2. Suppose you are a member of a church or Christian organization which does not have people who are capable and committed to leading others to maturity. How should you proceed?

Achievement Goals

1. After you have chosen a person with whom to work, at what date will you make the initial contact?

2. How frequently will you attempt to be with the person?

3. What will be your first step in ministry to this person?

Ideas for Further Research

1. Many tapes from the Foundation Library, 435 W. Boyd, Norman, Oklahoma 73069, are appropriate for this and other chapters. A catalog may be ordered from the above address.

2. Further helpful reading will be found in the books:

a. *New Testament Follow-up*, by Waylon B. Moore, pages 23–32.

b. *Jesus the Teacher*, by J. M. Price, pages 46–60.

Lesson 4
Consecration

Jesus' first requirement of his followers was a *willingness to obey him.* Without a doubt some of them were brilliant men, but brilliance was not one of our Lord's stipulations. The one thing our Lord insisted on was loyalty to him. Jesus continued to insist on this even when loyalty became increasingly difficult. He always claimed the right of setting forth the conditions and terms for being his disciple. But the fact that the disciples saw in him the spirit of obedience on which he insisted challenged them to stay with him.

Jesus knew that increased knowledge comes through obedience. He saw that learning truths about him would come in time, if only the disciples were willing to obey. One cannot be a leader who has not first learned to be a follower. He knew that development of character and purpose would come only through obedience. This is why he was willing to endure patiently many of their human failings as long as they were willing to obey him.

There is a critical need in the church today for a new commitment to the lordship of Christ. Stressing obedience at any cost must once again characterize the revolutionary message of the church. The people of God—preachers and laypersons alike—must cease to be complacent toward the commands of Christ. It is a situation which *must* be remedied. It may be that churches will have to begin a program of effective evangelism through a committed few who draw a small number of people to themselves and instill into this group the real meaning of obedience to Christ. Such action will be at least a start.

Learning Procedures

1. In Luke 9:57–62, three men came to Jesus as prospective followers. In your own words, describe the answer of Jesus to each. Then check pages 52–54.
   a._____
   b._____
   c._____

2. (a) What is your definition of a "disciple"?
   (b) What is Dr. Coleman's definition of the word?
3. What is the basic proof of real love for Christ?
4. "It must be remembered too that Jesus was making men to lead his church in conquest, and no one can ever be a _____ until he or she has learned to _____ a leader."
5. Three specific conditions for discipleship are mentioned in the Gospel of John. List them below as you look up the verse.
   a. John 8:31 _____
   b. John 13:35 _____
   c. John 15:8 _____

6. Jesus is to be Lord of every part of the life of a Christian. Listed below are some areas of the Christian life. Match them with the Scripture passage.

Possessions   A. Psalm 19:14
Time   B. Matthew 6:19–21
Speech   C. Colossians 3:18–21
Thought Life   D. Ephesians 5:15–16
Family Life   E. Philippians 4:8

Group Discussion and Activity

1. Discuss the meaning of the word *consecration.* Then call to memory as many New Testament instances as you can where consecration is exemplified.
2. Think over your knowledge of Christian acquaintances and see if you can find consecration exemplified in some of them.
3. On page 57 of the text, the author lists several passages which reflect Jesus' commitment to the will of God.

   John 4:34; John 5:30; John 15:10; Luke 22:42. Discuss what these meant to Jesus.

4. How does the lordship of Christ in one's life relate to witnessing?
5. If there is a widespread indifference to Christ among your Christian acquaintances, how can you proceed to change this situation?
6. Ask each group member to think about his or her personal Christian life. Then distribute five pipe cleaners to all present with instructions to twist and mold the pipe cleaners into what each believes best describes his or her Christian life. Allow about five

minutes for this activity. Then let each person explain the meanings portrayed in the arrangement of the pipe cleaners.

Achievement Goals

1. What does Jesus expect of me as a disciple?
2. The three passages listed below represent commands of Jesus to his followers. Read them and rate yourself on the chart below.

John 5:39   Luke 18:1   Matthew 4:19

I am obedient to these commands:

_____ consistently
_____ most of the time
_____ some of the time
_____ seldom
_____ never

3. Check yourself.

I seldom bear witness for Christ to others because:

_____ I am afraid I will offend someone.
_____ I am afraid the person will refuse to accept Christ.
_____ My life is not consistent as a Christian.
_____ I really do not think it is my responsibility to do it.
_____ I am afraid questions would be asked which I could not answer.
_____ I am not really sure others need Christ.
_____ I am not sure I have a real and vital relationship with Christ myself.

4. If you sense a need to do so, pause here and take time to pray a prayer of commitment to God regarding the above commands. Perhaps this prayer will reflect your feelings:

> O God, I confess that I have not been obedient to the commands of Christ as I should. Right now I commit myself to you anew, trusting you to so work in my life that I will be consistent in my study of your Word, in my prayer life, and in sharing the good news of Jesus with others. Amen.

5. Describe your plans for future provisions for personal Bible study and prayer.

_____

_____

6. If you know Christian friends who seem to be uninterested in obedience to Christ, here are some ways you might help them.
   a. Resolve to pray for them. "I will pray for the following Christians to grow in their devotion to Christ:

   _____

   _____

   _____."

   b. Cultivate a closer acquaintance with them, resolving, "I will cultivate a closer acquaintance with the following and endeavor to lead them into a deeper Christian life:

   _____

   _____

   _____."

Ideas for Further Research

1. Films:
   a. The film, *In His Steps*, produced by Ken Anderson Films, based on the famous novel of the same name, is a contemporary challenge to consecration.
   b. For teenagers, a series of filmstrips is published by Family Films, 2900 Queen Lane, Philadelphia, Pennsylvania 19129, entitled *Christian Teen-agers Spiritual Life Kit*.

2. A large number of books deal with this subject. One classic which every Christian should read is *The Christian's Secret of a Happy Life* by Hannah Whitall Smith.
3. There are several series of Bible study booklets which are helpful in leading one to profitable study of the Scriptures. Some of them are:
   a. *Ten Basic Steps Toward Christian Maturity*, Campus Crusade for Christ, Inc., Arrowhead Springs, San Bernardino, California.
   b. *Studies in Christian Living*, The Navigators, Colorado Springs, Colorado 80900.
   c. Set of six *Win or Grow Booklets*, Sunday School Board of the Southern Baptist Convention, Nashville, Tennessee.

Lesson 5
Impartation

The disciples could not help but be impressed with the fact that Jesus' life was a *life of giving*. He reflected the supreme demonstration of love as he literally gave his life away. They were constantly impressed that he loved a lost world. Jesus both understood and attempted to convey to them that he had been set apart for the evangelistic end of giving his life for the world's redemption. Through Jesus' demonstration, the disciples learned what real consecration meant. The fact that they learned self-giving was to be a factor by which the multitudes were to be convinced of the reality of the Gospel.

But the Twelve could never exhibit this kind of love apart from the impartation of Jesus' own life to them. This he did when he sent the Holy Spirit to indwell their lives. In giving the Holy Spirit to his followers, Jesus was also equipping them for evangelistic ministry. He frequently emphasized the fact that evangelism was not a human undertaking but a work of the Holy Spirit. His last hours with the Twelve were spent assuring them that the Holy Spirit would be adequate equipment for the evangelistic task. Thus it was that Pentecost was an absolute necessity before his followers could live, love, and serve in the ministry of evangelism.

And so it is today. Jesus' followers must have his life through the indwelling Spirit if his work is to be accomplished in and through the church. Only then will we be properly motivated. Only then will we possess the power to make him known. Only then will we demonstrate the self-sacrificing spirit necessary to effective evangelism.

Learning Procedures

1. Obedience is more than keeping laws. It is _____
   _____.

2. Jesus' constant renewal of his consecration to God expressed itself in _____.

3. The primary purpose for which Jesus sanctified himself was _____.

4. Jesus was God in _____; but the Spirit was God in _____.

5. Here is a comparison study of Jesus with the Twelve. There were things cherished by the disciples which Jesus refused. On the other hand, there were things they sought to escape which he willingly accepted. Below are seven words. In the two columns, list those cherished by the Twelve and the ones Jesus accepted willingly.

   physical satisfaction—poverty—humiliation
   prestige—death—popular acclaim—sorrow

Disciples	Jesus
_____	_____
_____	_____
_____	_____

6. List five things mentioned by the author which Jesus gave his followers:

_____   _____

_____   _____

_____

Group Discussion and Activity

1. Discuss the meaning of the word *sanctification* as it is found in John 17:18, 19. Then check page 63 in the text.
2. If your group is large enough, divide into three subgroups. Make the following assignments:
   a. Ask the first group to describe the work of the Holy Spirit in leading the Christian to be Christlike.
   b. Ask the second group to describe the work of and the necessity of the Holy Spirit for effective evangelism.
   c. Ask the third group to describe the conditions for the infilling with the Holy Spirit.

3. What one area in your life needs to be changed or strengthened in the light of today's study?

Achievement Goals

1. Get alone with God and make a list of every known sin or failure of which you are aware. Write them down, one by one, until everything the Holy Spirit has shown you to be wrong in your life is listed. Turn to 1 John 1:9 in your Bible. Confess the sins to God and write 1 John 1:9 across the sheet and destroy it.

2. In looking at your life, if you are aware of any area which has not been yielded to Christ, surrender that area of your life now.
3. Now pray the following prayer:

> Dear Father,
> I confess that there have been areas in my life which I have not yielded to you and as a result I have sinned against you. I thank you for complete forgiveness and right now yield every part of my life completely to you. By faith, I now claim the fullness of the Holy Spirit and thank you for taking control of my life and for filling me with him. Amen

Ideas for Further Research

1. A large number of tapes from The Foundation Library, mentioned in Lesson Three, deal with the subject of the Holy Spirit.
2. Many books have been written on the subject of the Holy Spirit. Two are *On Tiptoe with Joy!* by John T. Seamands, and *The Key to Triumphant Living*, by Jack R. Taylor.
3. The small pamphlet, *Have You Made the Wonderful Discovery of the Spirit-Filled Life?* published by Campus Crusade for Christ Inc., Arrowhead Springs, San Bernardino, California, is a helpful tool. A similar pamphlet, *How to Have a Spirit-Filled Life*, may be obtained from the Evangelism Division of the Baptist General Convention of Texas, Dallas, Texas 75201.

Lesson 6
Demonstration

It was a deliberate part of the strategy of Jesus to demonstrate the kind of life he planned for his people to live. Thus, the Twelve *observed in him the life they were to live and teach.* Everything about him was a demonstration for their sake and ours. He purposely let them see him talking with his Father in prayer. They saw what it did for him and yearned to know more of its power in their own lives. They were powerfully impressed with his mastery and use of the Old Testament Scriptures. Of particular importance is the fact that they watched as he won people to himself. They learned as they watched him practice before them what he wanted them to learn. Classes were always in session as the Master Teacher, in a natural manner, turned situation after situation into a learning opportunity.

Spiritual leaders are to emulate the plan of Jesus today. To effect this, we must be willing to demonstrate with our lives what we want others to learn. To accomplish this, we must be with those whom we want to lead. We must pray with them, help them in their study of the Scriptures, and take them with us as we attempt to win others to Christ. We will impart the way of life to others only as they see it in us. This

162

is the Master's method and its implementation is a must if others are to be adequately trained to do his work.

Learning Procedures

1. Though Jesus' life was a constant demonstration of how to live, the author singles out three particular areas of demonstration through which Jesus wanted to teach the Twelve. They were _____, _____, and _____.

2. Jesus' example is indication to his followers that they should know the Scriptures. According to the following verses, how may the Scriptures help us in our lives today?
   a. 1 Peter 2:2
   b. Psalm 119:105
   c. John 15:7

3. What lessons can you learn from the prayer life of Jesus?
   a. Matthew 14:23
   b. Mark 1:35
   c. Luke 6:12

Group Discussion and Activity

1. Compare Jesus' attitude toward the Scriptures with the statement of Paul in 2 Timothy 3:16–17.
2. Discuss the implications of: 1 Corinthians 11:1; Philippians 3:17; 2 Timothy 1:13; and Philippians 4:9.
3. Role-playing is the unrehearsed, dramatic enactment of a human conflict situation by two or more persons for the purpose of analysis by the group. Employing

the procedure of role-playing, select three members of the group to role-play the following:

The Problem: Here is a new Christian who wants to grow in the Lord. He is finding it difficult to pray. He doesn't know how to study his Bible and his first attempt to win someone to Christ was a miserable failure.

Let one person act out failure in these three areas. A second person, representing a lost friend, will be needed to act out failure in winning someone to Christ. Then, let a third person, representing a mature Christian, show through demonstration how having someone to teach in these areas can be of invaluable assistance.

Achievement Goals

1. If you have been working with a person, decide specifically how you are going to help teach this person to learn the following things·
   a. To pray
   b. To study the Bible effectively
   c. To share the Good News with others
   d. To be victorious in temptation
   e. To repent when one sins

2. I spend about this much time in Bible study and prayer each week:
   less than 1/2 hour
   1/2 to 1 hour
   1–2 hours
   2–3 hours
   more than 3 hours

3. Do you have a system of Scripture memory? If not, begin to commit at least one verse a week to memory.

Ideas for Further Research

1. A section of *Pastor Pastorum,* Latham, "The Schooling of the Apostles," pages 270–310, is a helpful study in demonstration.
2. The film, *Like a Mighty Army,* produced by Gospel Films Inc., of Muskegon, Michigan, is the story of the Coral Ridge Presbyterian Church of Fort Lauderdale, Florida. It strongly emphasizes the aspect of demonstration in teaching others to witness.
3. For assistance in memorizing Scripture verses, packets containing verses on cards may be obtained from The Navigators, Colorado Springs, Colorado 80900, and from the Billy Graham Evangelistic Association, Minneapolis, Minnesota 55440.

Lesson 7
Delegation

During the first year of Jesus' ministry, the disciples did little more than watch Jesus work. Though they were assigned responsibilities from the first, their initial involvement was with tasks which were quite menial. But this was a part of the Master's method. First, he led them into a vital relationship with God; then he showed them how he worked, and *only then* did he share with them the extent of their responsibilities. But he was always working with them with an eye toward the time they would take over his ministry.

Finally, after more than a year of training, Jesus realized they were ready for evangelistic work of their own. But Jesus was careful to thoroughly instruct them before he sent them out. The instructions are of great significance, since in them Jesus outlined explicitly what he had been implicitly teaching from the start. It is of special importance to notice that Jesus told them to concentrate their work on the more promising individuals who could carry on the work after they had gone. With assurance that they could expect hardship, he sent them, two by two, on their mission.

Involvement in the evangelistic task is an absolute imperative for every true follower of our Lord. Work assignments should be given to those whom we are training. These assignments should be of a practical nature at first, but always given with a view to preparing those we are leading for direct involvement in the redemptive ministry of our Lord.

Learning Procedures

1. Before telling the disciples they were to engage in world evangelism, Jesus' method included _____ and _____.

2. For a period of approximately _____, the disciples did little more than watch Jesus work.

3. What is the author's explanation as to why Jesus said to the Twelve, "Go not into the way of the Gentiles, and into any city of the Samaritans enter ye not: But go rather to the lost sheep of the house of Israel" (Matt. 10:5, 6)?

4. How does our author interpret the instruction of Jesus, "Into whatsoever city or village ye shall enter, search out who in it is worthy; and there abide till ye go forth"?

5. What indication is there that the witnessing efforts of the Twelve on their first mission were to some degree effective?

6. With the text and a New Testament in hand, match the following:

Luke 24:44–47   A. "Make disciples"
John 20:19–24   B. "Thomas was not with them"
Matthew 28:19   C. Promise of the Holy Spirit
Acts 1:8   D. "Feed my sheep"
John 21:15–17   E. "Into all the world"
Mark 16:15   F. "Repentance should be preached"

Group Discussion and Activity

1. Discuss this paragraph:
   Christian disciples are sent men and women—sent out in the same work of world evangelism to which the Lord was sent, and for which he gave his life. Evangelism is not an optional accessory to our life. It is the heartbeat of all that we are called to be and do. It is the commission of the church which gives meaning to all else that is undertaken in the name of Christ. With this purpose clearly in focus, everything which is done and said has glorious fulfillment of God's redemptive purpose—educational institutions, social programs, hospitals, church meetings of any kind—everything done in the name of Christ has its justification in fulfilling this mission.

2. Discuss the words of Jesus in Matthew 10:34–38.
   Think not that I came to send peace on earth: I came not to send peace, but a sword. For I am come to set a man at variance against his father, and the daughter against her mother, and the daughter-in-law against her mother-in-law. And a man's foes shall be they of his own household. He that loveth father or mother more than me is not worthy of me: and he that loveth son or daughter more than me is not worthy of me. And he that taketh not his cross and followeth after me, is not worthy of me.

   Now look at Dr. Coleman's comment on page 84.

3. Discuss the significance of the author's interpretation of Matthew 10:5, 6, as it relates to the beginning efforts of someone you might be training as a witness.

4. Look at the warnings of Jesus as to hardships the Twelve might experience. Consider them in the light of the passages: 1 Peter 2:21; Philippians 1:29; and 2 Timothy 3:12.

Achievement Goals

1. List some work assignments you might give to a new Christian with whom you are working.
2. If you have been working with a Christian in personal witnessing, let him or her begin to take over certain simpler parts of the conversation with a non-Christian.
3. Ask yourself the question, "Am I willing to witness for Jesus, even if it means bearing reproach for Christ's sake?"
4. If something seems to be hindering you from witnessing, check the list below. Be honest and face up to what it is. Trust God for continuous strength to overcome.
   False priorities
   Laziness
   Fear
   Prejudice against evangelism
   Sins of the flesh
Above all, make yourself *available* to God.

Ideas for Further Research

1. Books:
   a. *Every Member Evangelism,* by J. E. Conant, is a powerful book encouraging delegation of the responsibility of witnessing.
   b. A section of *The Training of the Twelve,* by A. B. Bruce, "First Attempts at Evangelism," pages 99–119, is very appropriate

Lesson 8
Supervision

Though he had entrusted the Twelve with some evangelistic responsibility, Jesus did not yet look on them as finished products who were ready to graduate. Even in the limited amount of redemptive work in which they had engaged, *they needed supervision.* Thus, Jesus got with them following their tours of service to hear their reports and to share with them his knowledge about difficulties they might have encountered or victories they might have won. And indeed, this is no isolated incident. Through constant fellowship with them, Jesus was perpetually keeping check on the Twelve. Throughout his ministry with them, the experiences of the disciples, whether they represented success or failure, were raw materials for Jesus to use in teaching and making application. He was ever alert to their actions and reactions, keeping in mind that his supervision was one more step in equipping them for ministry. When he finally did leave them to go back to the Father, he promised the Holy Spirit to them to continue to supervise their work.

In equipping people for evangelistic ministry today, we cannot presume that merely showing people how will result in the work being done. Nor can we assume that the successful completion of one task reflects a readiness on the part of the person being trained to be on his or her own. Until disciples have been brought to a place of maturity, close supervision is still a necessity.

Learning Procedures

1. Compare the report session of the Twelve with that of the seventy.
2. What was Jesus' reaction to the report of the seventy?
3. List one instance where Jesus used failure on the part of the Twelve to bring out truth they needed to know.
4. The author uses three words to describe Jesus' plan of teaching. They are _____, _____, and _____.

Group Discussion and Activity

1. The author uses the term *world conquest* twice in this chapter. What, in your opinion, is meant by this?
2. Discuss this paragraph:

   When will we learn the lessons of Christ not to be satisfied merely with the firstfruits of those who are sent out to witness? Disciples must be brought to maturity. There can be no substitute for total victory, and our field is the world. We have not been called to hold the fort, but to storm the heights. It is in this light that the final step in Jesus' strategy of evangelism can be understood.

3. Someone you have been working with has been rebuffed. It could be in one of several ways. Discuss how you could encourage her when she encounters the following:

   a. On introducing herself, she had a door slammed in her face.

    b. On sharing the Good News, someone sincerely asked, "But how do you know it is really true?"

    c. "I don't believe there is a God."

    d. "Isn't Christian experience only psychological?"

4. Let this meeting be a report session. Ask and answer the following questions.

    a. Whom have you met this week who needs help?

    b. What have you done about it?

    c. Think of three people—family, friends, business associates, shut-ins, etc.—to whom you will demonstrate Christian concern this week. You will take a few minutes to share with them or will perform some planned act of kindness toward them. Record the act, whether done by phone, in person, or by letter. Write down what happened.

Achievement Goals

1. Have a planned report session after sending your friend out to do some piece of Christian work.

2. Make a list of discouraging difficulties a new witness might face and be prepared to help him or her with them.

Ideas for Further Research

1. Gospel Films has produced four Teaching Training Films on Lay Witnessing as it is done in the Coral Ridge Presbyterian Church, Fort Lauderdale, Florida. The third of these, *On the Job Training*, emphasizes this aspect of teaching.

2. The book, *Evangelism Explosion*, by D. James Kennedy, has a wholesome emphasis on supervision.

Lesson 9
Reproduction

The ultimate goal of Jesus for his disciples was that *his life be reproduced in them and through them into the lives of others.* The fact that the group of men he led was small made little difference. If they were adequately trained, they would produce lives which would be like theirs. Lives like these would produce the same kind of fruit until Jesus could envision the whole world hearing his message. The ultimate victory would come through their faithful witness of him. His gospel would conquer as they reproduced and taught their disciples to reproduce. Reproduction was our Lord's desire for the Twelve but multiplication was the ultimate end.

Today, as then, the test of an evangelistic program is not the number of people who are being reached for first-time decisions. The real test is: *Are those who are being reached reaching others?* Is our fruit bearing fruit? Are we only making converts—or are we building leaders who can in turn build other leaders?

The early church, with its incorporation of the plan of winning and developing men to reproduce, proved the workability of Jesus' plan; but ensuing centuries witnessed the virtual abandonment of it for one of mass recruitment. *The need of the hour is a return to the kind of evangelism which majors*

*in people winning other people to Christ and building those they
have won into disciples who can win and build others.*

Learning Procedures

1. Answer the following true-or-false questions.
   a. Reproduction is the chief end of evangelism.

   _____

   b. Mass recruitment by the church seems to have
      worked to the detriment of the Christian move-
      ment. _____
   c. The principle of Jesus in evangelism has not been
      recaptured by the church to any great extent since
      the fourth century. _____
   d. The real command in Matthew 28:19–20 is to
      make disciples. _____

2. Matthew 9:36–38 pictures an experience of Jesus seeing vast multitudes of people. Describe his response
   to this.
   What did he encourage his disciples to pray?
3. What is the ultimate evaluation of our life and witness as to the redemptive purposes of God?
4. The test of any work of evangelism thus is not
   _____, but in _____.
5. Similarly, the criteria on which a church should measure its success are not _____, nor _____,
   but rather _____.
6. Evangelism is not done by _____ but by
   _____.
7. The new evangelism needed is not better methods
   but better _____.

Group Discussion and Activity

1. Dr. Coleman speaks of Jesus' foreseeing the day "when the gospel of salvation in his name would be proclaimed convincingly to every creature." Discuss the prospects for this happening in our generation.

2. Study thoroughly John 15:1–16. Note how many times the word *fruit* is used in these passages. Discuss what Jesus meant by this word. Then see page 100. Notice verse 16 where Jesus talks about fruit remaining. What is meant by this?

3. Discuss the paragraph on pages 102–103:

   What really counts in the ultimate perpetuation of our work is the faithfulness with which our converts go out and make leaders out of their converts, not simply more followers. Surely we want to win our generation for Christ, and to do it now, but this is not enough. Our work is never finished until it has assured its continuation in the lives of those redeemed by the Evangel.

4. Discuss what you would do about winning the following people:

   a. Next door there lives a man who would like churches to be destroyed. He is very open in his hostility to Christians and believes they are a detriment to society. Sometimes his hatred almost turns into a rage. What, if anything, could be done to reach him for Christ? Do you honestly believe he could be saved? Read Acts 8:3; 9:1–6.

   b. Next door lives a man who is extremely religious. He prays, helps the poor, and leads his family to be religious, yet, he has never come to know Christ personally. What would your attitude toward him be? What would you do to reach this man for Christ? Do you believe he could become a Christian? Read Acts 10.

Achievement Goals

1. You have been working with a woman with a view to leading her to become a witness. As she goes with you, let her have more and more of the conversation until ultimately she carries it all the way, even to the point of asking a person to accept Christ. If the person with whom you have been working is not to this point, stay with her until she is.

The person with whom I am working is:

_____ able to enter into introductory conversation and introduce Christ into the conversation.

_____ able to share the gospel intelligently, but not ready to ask for a commitment.

_____ able to share the gospel and lead a person to a decision.

2. Your goal is not only to help individuals with whom you have been working to lead someone to Christ. You have also been working toward their being able to take the person they have led to Christ and lead him or her to a place of maturity. Be sure individuals with whom you have been working understand that.

Ideas for Further Research

1. Several films have very poignant messages relating to the content of this chapter. Among them:

a. *No Time to Wait*, Augsburg Publishing House, 426 South Fifth Street, Minneapolis, Minnesota 55415.

b. *Born to Witness*, Family Films, 5823 Santa Monica Blvd., Hollywood, California 90038.

c. *The Gospel Blimp*, Gospel Films, Muskegon, Michigan 49440.

d. *How to Witness*, Broadman Films, Sunday School Board of the Southern Baptist Convention, Nashville, Tennessee.

e. Part I and Part II of the Coral Ridge teaching training films on Lay Witnessing: *Challenge to Witness* and *The Gospel Presentation*, Gospel Films.

2. Tapes #3 and #4 of the Coral Ridge Cassettes, David C. Cook Publishing Company, Elgin, Illinois, are extremely helpful here.

Lesson 10
The Master and Your Plan
—Step One

There is an old story, imagined by someone, of Jesus ascending back to heaven and encountering the angel Gabriel shortly after he arrived. Gabriel was terribly interested in what our Lord had been doing on earth. Jesus responded by explaining that while on earth, he had died on a cross to save men from their sins and had been raised up by God's power. He had now returned to heaven to take his place at God's right hand to intercede for those whom he had come to save. Jesus concluded by saying that it was his desire that all people everywhere hear the message of what he had done for them. Gabriel asked, "And what is your plan for getting this done?" Our Lord responded, "I have left the message in the hands of a dozen or so men. I am trusting them to spread it everywhere." Somewhat surprised, Gabriel exclaimed, "Twelve men! And what if they fail?" Jesus is reported to have said, "I have no other plan."

Regardless of the imaginary aspect of it, the main point of the story is true. Jesus did leave the task of evangelizing to a small number of people. But they so thoroughly trained others to bear effective witness that soon large numbers of trained disciples were sharing the truth about Jesus all over Jerusalem, Judea, Samaria, Galilee, and ultimately to the uttermost parts of the earth.

His plan, revolving around trained disciples who are winning and training others to win and train, has never changed.

Learning Procedures

1. As you work with a person, list here some opportunities you might have of getting together with that person for training in discipleship.

2. In working with a person or a small group, what are some activities in which you might engage when you are together?

3. What are some possible assignments you might give to a person you are helping to disciple?

   a. Early or first assignments.

   b. Assignments to give as the person matures in the Lord.

4. At what point would you explain your strategy to a person with whom you have been working?

Group Activity and Discussion

1. Make this session a report session. Discuss: Whom have I met this week that needs help? What have I done to help someone this week? What was the response?

2. Discuss: "Better to give a year or so to one or two men or women who learn what it means to conquer for Christ than to spend a lifetime with a congregation just keeping the program going." Ask the group to agree or disagree. What are the implications of this

statement? What is involved in the phrase, "conquer for Christ"?

3. On page 115, Dr. Coleman speaks of some people who think the standards of discipleship are too high and fall by the way. Think of some people in the New Testament who did. See Acts 1:25; 1 Timothy 4:10; 2 Timothy 1:15; 2 Timothy 1:19, 20. What will your response be if some with whom you are working prove to be unteachable, unwilling to pay the price, and fall by the way?

4. In your prayer period, as a group, pray for each person in the group by name.

Personal Achievement

1. Write out your personal testimony about becoming a Christian in approximately 150–200 words. It should be outlined something like this: *First,* what your life without Christ was like. *Second,* how you became a Christian. *Third,* what life has been like since you received Christ. Steer away from heavy theological words and clichés which mean nothing to most people who are not Christians. Major on what Christ means to you and is doing for you today. Commit this to memory.

2. You are a Sunday school teacher. Each one in your class is a Christian and attends with some degree of regularity. You prepare lessons faithfully, visit absentees, and occasionally plan a party or outing for your class. As yet, nothing outstanding has happened in the lives of members of your class. How do you plan to proceed with the Master Plan? Look at the chapter headings again. Proceed on the basis of the contents of the chapter headings.

3. You are a part of the bus ministry of your church. A child who rides your bus makes a profession of faith. How will you go about your ministry of follow-up?
4. What are the primary lessons you have learned in the preceding nine chapters? How have you begun to put them into practice? What are your plans for the future?

Ideas for Further Research

1. Film IV of the Coral Ridge training series, *Follow-Up*, Gospel Films, Muskegon, Michigan.
2. The book, *Evangelism Explosion*, by D. James Kennedy, has an excellent section on follow-up.
3. The pamphlet, *Christ in You*, published by InterVarsity Press, is good material for follow-up of a new Christian.
4. The booklet, *How to Have a Quiet Time*, published by The Navigators, Colorado Springs, Colorado, is pertinent in follow-up.
5. A series of follow-up tapes may be obtained from the Coral Ridge Presbyterian Church, 1901 Northeast 50th Street, Fort Lauderdale, Florida.

Lesson 11
The Master and Your Plan
—Step Two

Recently I saw one of the most forceful demonstrations of the importance of spiritual multiplication I can remember. Two men were asked to come and stand at the front of a very crowded auditorium. Both of them represented pastors who win people to Christ through personal witnessing. One of the two (perhaps the more aggressive witness) represented the pastor who wins many people to Christ personally, but who is so busy winning people he never takes time to train anyone to do it. The other (perhaps less dynamic in his own personal evangelism) takes time to train those whom he wins to win others. He goes even one step further and trains them to train the ones they have won.

The demonstration began when each of the two men went out into the congregation and brought back with them to the front of the auditorium another person who represented someone they had won to Christ. The first pastor continued to do this, to bring them one by one, until after ten trips he had ten others with him at the front representing those he had won to Christ. The second pastor, who was training those he had won, went into the congregation along with the first person he had won and trained, and each of them brought back one. This made four. The four won to Christ and trained went out and each brought back one and there were eight. This man and those whom he had trained made only five trips into the congregation. But thirty-two people stood with him after five trips in contrast to the ten people who stood with the other. Had this pastor and those he trained made ten trips into the congregation, 1,024 people would have stood with him! The difference is the difference between addition and multiplication. *It is more important to train a soul winner than to win a soul.* The church must return to the principle of multiplication if we are to make the impact on this lost world our Lord would have us to make.

Learning Procedures

1. A number of concepts are included in spiritual growth which leads to maturity. Some of them are found in the verses below. Look at the verse and see if you can determine what the particular aspect of growth is.
   1 John 5:13
   Ephesians 4:14
   Ephesians 4:13
   Matthew 4:19
   Matthew 28:19

2. Here is one for those who love arithmetic. Suppose you were the only Christian in the world. In the next six months you win one person and train him to win and train others. At the end of six months there are two Christians, both capable of winning and training. Each of you wins and trains one in the next six months and then there are four. Each wins and trains one in the next months and there are eight. Follow-

ing this procedure, how many people would be won to Christ over a period of sixteen years? Don't lose heart in working it.

Answer:

Group Discussion and Activity

1. Determine the number of people who were added to your church by profession of faith last year. Then determine the total membership of your church. Divide the number of people added by profession into the total membership. The quotient (figure which represents the answer) answers how many members it took to win one person to Christ and to an open confession of him in your church last year.

2. Now, figure how many people would be won to Christ if every member won one person in the next year. What would your approximate membership be at the end of the year? If each of these won someone during the next year, how many would be won?

3. Bring some old newspapers with you to the group meeting. Think for a minute about someone who is away from God and whom you would like to see get right with God. Concentrate on what you believe the person's basic needs are. What are the anxieties, hangups, tensions? Put yourself in his or her shoes. Take a few minutes to take the newspaper and tear out of it every headline, every ad, every picture, and everything that reminds you of your friend who is not right with God. Discard the remainder of the paper and using the materials you have torn out, describe your friend in two minutes to the rest of the group.

Personal Achievement

1. Read Ephesians 4:11, 12 in a modern translation of the New Testament. Paul makes it clear that evangelism is to be a part of the life of every member of Christ's church. Write below your own honest feeling about being called to take part in the ministry of evangelism.

   Whether your feelings are negative or positive, attempt to explain why you feel this way.

2. Make a list of reasons why working with others to build them in the faith is difficult.

   How can these difficulties best be overcome?

3. If you have attempted to win people to Christ and they have declined your invitation to receive him, what reasons did they give? Write an analysis of your witness, including strengths and weaknesses.

Lesson 12
The Master and Your Plan
—Step Three

Recently I visited one of the fastest growing churches in the United States. I have never been any more impressed by the combination of evangelistic outreach and apparent spiritual depth than I was with this congregation. The evolution of the program of evangelism in this church is interesting. Chronologically, it began when the pastor preached to his congregation that each of them should witness. This produced no witnesses. Then he held classes or study courses. The same result—no witnesses. Then the pastor began to take one man with him as he bore witness to Jesus. This man watched over a period of weeks as the pastor led people to Christ. Soon, the man got the idea and began to witness himself. He began to take a person with him and the pastor took another, so soon there were four. As people were won, they were trained to win others. The four became eight, the eight, sixteen, until now there are approximately five hundred people in that church who can intelligently share their faith with others. It's no wonder that members of that church led to Christ over one thousand people last year! *They have learned the secret of multiplication.* They are following the Master's plan of evangelism.

Learning Procedures

1. The New Testament calls attention to a number of ways in which believers can be followed up. Listed below are four Scripture verses. List the particular method of follow-up suggested by the verse.
   a. Acts 15:36
   b. Philippians 1:9
   c. 1 Thessalonians 3:1, 2
   d. Galatians 6:11

2. Nothing is more vital in follow-up ministry than prayer. Notice the content of two of Paul's prayers for believers which are recorded in Ephesians. List the requests he makes in their behalf.
   a. Ephesians 1:15–20
   b. Ephesians 3:14–19

Group Discussion and Activity

1. Discuss: What long-range goals are there in the organizational structure of our church which will help us incorporate the principles of the Master Plan? What short-range goals should we have for this year?
2. Brainstorming is a method of problem solving in which group members suggest in rapid-fire order all the possible solutions they can think of. Criticism is ruled out. Evaluation of ideas comes later. Use the brainstorming method with the clause "variety and resourcefulness in a new and bold approach."

3. One of the subheads in the last chapter is titled "Methods Will Vary." Discuss a variety of methods which might be employed by either an individual or a small group.

4. If you are a part of outreach ministry to a convalescent home, jail, or detention home, discuss possible ways of leading those who make decisions to maturity.

Personal Achievement

1. If you have been working with an individual, suggest some people to whom he or she might begin witnessing. Some of these would be:

2. Here are some suggestions as to "How to have a quiet time." Share them with those with whom you have been working.

   a. Have a definite time. Choose the most appropriate time for you.

   b. Have a definite place. A place secluded from noise or interruptions is best. Be *alone* with God.

   c. Have a definite plan in mind. First, make a list of requests for which to pray. Then, spend some of the time studying the Bible.

3. Undoubtedly, by now, you have had resistance from the enemy in your efforts to win and mature people. Those with whom you are working also experience this. Satan will tempt you and them along this line, "What do you mean trying to lead someone in the Christian life? You are too unworthy for this. You are not even sure of your own salvation." Learn to use the Word of God to meet his attacks. Meet this onslaught with 1 John 5:11–13 ·

Next, he might whisper to you, "You may be a Christian, all right, but look at the areas in which you have failed since becoming a Christian." Respond to this temptation with 1 John 1:9.

Third, he will tell you, that though you are a Christian, you are much too weak to resist temptation. On this occasion remember 1 Corinthians 10:13.

Lesson 13
The Master and Your Plan
—Step Four

The population of our world is increasing at an unbelievable rate. Every time a clock ticks off a second, world population has increased by two. This means there will be almost 200,000 more people in our world tomorrow than there are today, according to United Nations estimates. In one generation, if the trend continues, world population will exceed seven billion.

While the people-rate increases at the speed of a rocket, the rate at which these people are being reached with the gospel virtually proceeds at the pace of an ox cart. The percentage of evangelical Christians in our world has grown smaller and smaller in recent decades. A famous evangelist has said, "We are not winning our world for Christ—we are losing our world for Christ." There is but one hope to stem the tide: *That is a return on the part of the church to the Master's plan of evangelism.*

What is the plan of your life, the one life God has entrusted to you? Are you investing it in a ministry which gives priority to working with people? Do you have your person or your small group in whom and through whom you are multiplying yourself? There are no worthwhile shortcuts in world evangelization. We must follow his plan, even at the price of being denied impressive statistical reports for the present. But with an eye to the future and a vision of his name proclaimed to every person, commit yourself anew to Jesus to do his work his way.

Learning Procedures

1. The New Testament describes new or immature Christians in terms of _____.

2. What does the above term suggest as far as the need of follow-up is concerned? Check the following verses and list some needs of new or immature Christians.
   a. Ephesians 4:14
   b. 1 Thessalonians 2:7, 11
   c. 1 Peter 2:2

3. Paul and Barnabas spent approximately five months in the city of Thessalonica on his second missionary journey. Describe this church on the basis of 1 Thessalonians 1.
   How could this kind of church come from such a brief ministry?

4. We have been working toward leading believers to spiritual maturity. Listed below are verses which suggest some marks of a mature believer. List them.
   a. 2 Corinthians 5:7
   b. 1 Thessalonians 5:18
   c. 2 Corinthians 9:7
   d. 1 John 3:16, 17
   e. Ephesians 6:18
   f. Hebrews 5:14

Group Discussion and Activity

1. What small groups already exist in your church which could implement the principles of the Master Plan? List them on a blackboard.
2. With your books open to pages 108–115 let each one list in outline form the points considered essential for individuals to use if they are to disciple others. Discuss your findings.
3. Freely discuss difficulties you have had in witnessing and how they may be alleviated. Close with prayer for each other.

Personal Achievement

1. If you have had the privilege recently of leading someone to Christ, describe below in some detail your plans for helping to lead the person to spiritual maturity.
2. Briefly describe your plans for a permanent strategy of evangelism for your own life.

Answers to Learning Procedures

(Page numbers referred to are from *The Master Plan of Evangelism.*)

Lesson 1

3. Principles
4. the Gospel records
5. (a) F (b) F (c) F

Lesson 2

1. (a) Judas (b) 500 (c) John
2. (a) p. 27 (b) p. 27 (c) p. 29 (d) pp. 29–30
3. (a) F (b) F (c) T

Lesson 3

2. (a) p. 41 (b) p. 42 (c) p. 47
3. (a) more (b) 1/2 (c) the disciples

Lesson 4

2. (b) p. 52 **3.** John 14:21 **4.** p. 58 **6.** B, D, A, E, C

Lesson 5

1. p. 61 **2.** p. 63 **3.** p. 63 **4.** p. 66 **5.** pp. 62, 63 **6.** p. 61

Lesson 6

1. pp. 71–75

Lesson 7

1. p. 79 **2.** p. 80 **3.** p. 81 **4.** p. 82 **5.** p. 86 **6.** F, B, A, C, D, E

Lesson 8
1. pp. 89–90 2. p. 90 3. p. 91 4. p. 94

Lesson 9
1. (a) F (b) T (c) T (d) T 3. p. 101 4. p. 103 5. p. 103
6. p. 105

Lesson 10
1. p. 110 2. pp. 110–112 3.(a) p. 112 (b) p. 113 4. p. 114

Lesson 11
1. assurance
doctrinal stability
Christlikeness
winning others
discipling others
2. 4,294,967,296

Lesson 12
1. (a) personal contact
(b) prayer
(c) sending someone else
(d) letters

Lesson 13
1. Babes
2. (a) protection from false doctrine
(b) loving care and concern
(c) food, the milk of the Word
4. (a) living by faith
(b) giving thanks in everything
(c) cheerful giving
(d) compassion toward others
(e) praying always
(f) discernment

Selected Bibliography in Basic Evangelism and Discipleship

Adsit, Christopher. *Personal Disciple-Making* (Here's Life, 1989).

Aldrich, Joseph. *Life-Style Evangelism* (Multnomah, 1981).

_____. *Gentle Persuasion*, (Multnomah, 1988).

Allen, Roland. *Missionary Methods: St. Paul's or Ours* (World Dominion Press, 1953).

_____. *Spontaneous Expansion of the Church and the Causes Which Hinder It* (World Dominion Press, 1949).

Anderson, Leith. *A Church for the Twenty-first Century* (Bethany House, 1992).

Arn, Win and Charles. *The Master's Plan for Making Disciples* (Church Growth Press, 1982).

Augsburger, Myron S. *Invitation to Discipleship* (Herald, 1969).

Bayly, Joseph. *The Gospel Blimp* (Zondervan, 1966).

Belben, Howard. *The Mission of Jesus* (NavPress, 1985).

Bisagno, John R. *How To Build An Evangelistic Church* (Broadman, 1972).

Boer, Harry R. *Pentecost and Missions* (Eerdmans).

Brooks, Hal. *Follow-up Evangelism* (Broadman, 1972).

Bonar, Horatius. *Words to Winners of Souls,* rev. ed. (American Tract Society, 1950).

Bounds, E. M. *Preacher and Prayer* (London: Marshall Brothers, 1912).

Brengle, S. L. *The Soul-Winner's Secret,* 6th ed. (Salvation Army, 1920).

Bright, Bill. *Witnessing Without Fear* (Here's Life, 1987).

Briscoe, Stuart. *Everyday Discipleship for Ordinary People* (Victor, 1988).

Brown, Stanley C. *Evangelism in the Early Church* (Eerdmans, 1963).

Bruce, A. B. *The Training of the Twelve* (Keats, 1979 [1871]).

Chafer, Lewis Sperry. *True Evangelism* (Marshall, Morgan & Scott, 1919).

195

Cho, Paul Y. *More Than Numbers* (Word, 1984).

Choose Ye This Day: How to Effectively Proclaim the Gospel Message (World Wide, 1989).

Coleman, Lyman. *Serendipity Bible for Groups* (Zondervan, 1988).

_____. *Encyclopedia of Serendipity* (Serendipity House, 1976).

Coleman, Robert E. *The Master Plan of Discipleship* (Revell, 1987).

_____. *Mind of the Master* (Revell, 1977).

_____. *They Meet the Master* (Christian Outreach, 1973).

_____. *The Heartbeat of Evangelism* (NavPress, 1985).

_____. *The Spark That Ignites* (World Wide, 1989).

_____, ed. *Evangelism on the Cutting Edge* (Revell, 1986).

_____. *The Great Commission Lifestyle* (Revell, 1992).

Coppedge, Allan. *The Biblical Principles of Discipleship* (Zondervan, 1989).

Cosgrove, Francis M. *Essentials of Discipleship* (NavPress, 1980).

Dawson, David. *Equipping the Saints* (Greenville, TX, 1982).

Dawson, John. *Taking Over Cities for God* (Creation House, 1989).

Drummond, Lewis. *Leading Your Church in Evangelism* (Broadman, 1975).

_____. *The Awakening That Must Come* (Broadman, 1989).

_____. *The Word of the Cross: A Contemporary Theology of Evangelism* (Broadman, 1992).

Eims, Leroy. *The Lost Art of Disciple Making* (Zondervan, 1978).

_____. *Be the Leader You Were Meant to Be* (Victor, 1975).

_____. *Disciples in Action* (Victor, 1981).

Eisenman, Tom. *Everyday Evangelism* (IV, 1988).

Engel, James F. and H. Wilbert Norton. *What's Gone Wrong with the Harvest?* (Zondervan, 1975).

Evangelistic Preaching: A Self-Study Course in Creating and Presenting Messages that Call People to Christ (World Wide, 1990).

Fernando, Ajith. *Leadership Lifestyle* (Tyndale, 1984).

Finney, Charles. *Lectures on Revivals of Religion*, reprint (Revell, 1958).

Fish, Roy. *Every Member Evangelism for Today* (Harper & Row, 1976 [1922]).

Ford, Leighton. *Good News is for Sharing* (David C. Cook, 1977).

_____. *The Christian Persuader* (Harper & Row, 1966).

Friedeman, Matt. *The Master Plan of Teaching* (Victor, 1990).

Fryling, Alice, ed. *Disciple Makers' Handbook* (InterVarsity, 1989).

George, Carl. *Prepare Your Church For the Future* (Revell, 1991).

Graham, Billy. *A Biblical Standard for Evangelists* (World Wide, 1984).

_____. *The Billy Graham Christian Worker's Handbook* (World Wide, 1981).

Green, Michael. *Evangelism in the Local Church* (Tyndale, 1992).

Hadidian, Allen. *Successful Discipling* (Moody, 1979).

Hanks, Billie, Jr., and William A. Shell, eds. *Discipleship: The Best Writings of the Most Experienced Disciple Makers* (Zondervan, 1981).

Hanks, Billie, Jr. *Everyday Evangelism* (Zondervan, 1984).

Harrison, E. Myers, and Walter L. Wilson. *How To Win Souls* (Van Kampen, 1952).

Hartman, Doug, and Doug Sutherland. *A Guidebook to Discipleship* (Harvest 1976).

Heck, Joel D. *The Art of Sharing Your Faith* (Revell, 1989).

_____. *Make Disciples: Evangelism Program of the Eighties* (Concordia, 1984).

Hendricks, Howard. *Say It With Love* (Gospel Light, 1972).

Hendrix, John, and Lloyd Hoseholder, eds. *The Equipping of Disciples* (Broadman, 1977).

Henrichsen, Walter A. *Disciples Are Made, Not Born* (Victor, 1975).

Hull, Bill. *Jesus Christ, Disciple-Maker* (NavPress, 1984).

_____. *The Disciple-Making Pastor* (Revell, 1988).

_____. *The Disciple-Making Church* (Revell, 1990).

Hunter, George. *The Contagious Congregation* (Abingdon, 1980).

Huston, Sterling W. *Crusade Evangelism and the Local Church* (World Wide, 1984).

Hyde, Douglas. *Dedication and Leadership* (University of Notre Dame Press, 1966).

Jacks, Bob and Betty. *Your Home a Lighthouse* (NavPress, 1986).

Jones, Charles E. *Life is Tremendous* (Tyndale, 1968).

Kennedy, James. *Evangelism Explosion* 3d. ed. (Tyndale, 1983).

Kincaid, Ron. *A Celebration of Disciplemaking* (Victor, 1990).

Kuhne, Gary W. *The Dynamics of Personal Follow-Up* (Eerdmans, 1976).

_____. *Dynamics of Discipleship Training* (Zondervan, 1978).

Kunz, Marilyn, and Catherine Schell. *How to Start a Neighborhood Bible Study* (Tyndale, 1970).

Latham, Henry. *Pastor Pastorum* (Deighton Bell & Co., 1910).

Let the Earth Hear His Voice, ed. by J. D. Douglas (World Wide, 1975). Addresses and papers given at the International Congress on World Evangelism in Lausanne, Switzerland.

Let the Church Obey His Voice. Four reproducible notebooks issued by the American Festival of Evangelism in Kansas City in 1981

Lewis, Larry. *Organize to Evangelize* (Victor, 1980).

Little, Paul E. *How to Give Away Your Faith* (InterVarsity, 1966).

MacDonald, William. *True Discipleship* (Walterick, 1962).

Mainhood, Beth. *Reaching Your World* (NavPress, 1986).

Mayhall, Carole. *From the Heart of a Woman: Basic Discipleship from a Woman's Viewpoint* (NavPress, 1976).

Mayhall, Jack. *Discipleship* (Victor, 1984).

McCloskey, Mark. *Tell It Often—Tell It Well* (Here's Life, 1986).

McClung, Floyd. *Basic Discipleship* (InterVarsity, 1990).

McGavran, Donald. *Understanding Church Growth*. 3d ed., revised and edited by Peter Wagner (Eerdmans, 1990).

Miller, John C. *Evangelism and Your Church* (Presbyterian and Reformed, 1980).

Miles, Delos. *Master Principles of Evangelism* (Broadman, 1982).

Moore, Waylon. *Multiplying Disciples* (NavPress, 1981).

_____. *New Testament Follow-Up* (Eerdmans, 1972).

Morgan, G. Campbell. *The Great Physician* (Revell, 1937).

Neighbor, Ralph W. *Target Group Evangelism* (Broadman, 1975).

_____. *Where Do We Go From Here* (Torch, 1990).

Nicholas, Ron, and others. *Good Things Come in Small Groups* (InterVarsity, 1990).

Ogden, Greg. *The New Reformation* (Zondervan, 1990).

One Race, One Gospel, One Task ed. by Carl F. H. Henry and W. Stanley Mooneyham, 2 vols. (World Wide, 1967). Papers and addresses given at the World Congress on Evangelism in Berlin in 1966.

Olford, Stephen. *Lord, Open the Heavens* (Shaw, 1980).

_____. *The Secret of Soul-Winning* (Moody, 1963).

Ortez, Juan C. *The Disciple* (Creation House, 1970–1989).

_____. *Call to Discipleship* (Logos, 1975).

Palmer, Bernard and Marjorie Palmer. *How Churches Grow* (Bethany, 1976).

Packer, J. I. *Evangelism and the Sovereignty of God* (InterVarsity, 1961).

Peace, Richard. *Small Group Evangelism* (InterVarsity, 1985).

Pentecost, J. Dwight. *Design for Discipleship* (Zondervan, 1971).

Perspectives on the World Christian Movement, ed. Steven C. Hawthorne and Ralph D. Winter (William Carey Library, 1981).

Petersen, Jim. *Evangelism as a Lifestyle* (NavPress, 1980).

Phillips, Keith. *The Making of a Disciple* (Revell, 1981).

Poterski, Donald C. *Reinventing Evangelism* (InterVarsity, 1989).

Powell, Paul W. *Dynamic Discipleship* (Broadman Press, 1984).

Pratney, Winkie. *Youth Aflame* (Communication Foundation, 1974).

Prince, Matthew. *Winning Through Caring* (Baker, 1981).

Prior, David. *Parish Renewal at the Grassroots* (Zondervan, 1983).

Rainer, Thom S., ed. *Evangelism in the Twenty-First Century* (Harold Shaw, 1989).

Ratz, Calvin, Frank Tillapaugh, and Myron Augsburger. *Mastering Outreach and Evangelism* (Multnomah, 1990).

Robertson, Roy. *The Timothy Principle* (NavPress, 1986).

Rudnick, Milton L. *Speaking the Gospel Through the Ages* (Concordia, 1984).

Salter, Darious. *What Really Matters in Ministry* (Baker, 1990).

Sanny, Lorne. *Marks of a Disciple* (NavPress, 1975).

Schweer, G. William. *Personal Evangelism for Today* (Broadman, 1984).

Segovia, Fernando F. *Discipleship in the New Testament* (Fortress, 1985).

Shaver, Charles "Chic." *Conserve the Converts* (Beacon Hill, 1976).

———. *The Bible Speaks to Me About My Witness* (Beacon Hill, 1991).

Shoemaker, Samuel A. *Revive Thy Church Beginning With Me* (Harper & Brothers, 1948).

———. *With the Holy Spirit and With Fire* (Harper & Brothers, 1960).

Shumate, Charles R. *On the Grow* (Walner, 1984).

Smith, Bailey. *Real Evangelism* (Broadman, 1978).

Smith, Glenn C., ed. *Evangelizing Adults* (Paulist National Catholic Evangelization Association and Tyndale House, 1985).

Smith, Oswald. *The Passion for Souls* (Marshall, Morgan & Scott, 1950).

Snyder, Howard. *The Problem of Wineskins: Church Structure in a Technological Age* (InterVarsity 1975).

Spurgeon, Charles H. *The Soul Winner*, ed. David Otis Fuller (Zondervan, 1984).

Stott, John R. W. *Our Guilty Silence* (Hodder & Stoughton, 1967).

———. *Personal Evangelism* (InterVarsity, 1970).

Street, R. Alan. *The Effective Invitation* (Revell, 1984).

Sweazy, George E. *Effective Evangelism*, rev. ed. (Harper & Brothers, 1976).

Tam, Stanley. *Every Christian A Soul Winner* (Thomas Nelson, 1975).

Taylor, Mendall. *Exploring Evangelism* (Beacon Hill, 1964).

The Calling of An Evangelist, ed. by J. D. Douglas (World Wide, 1987). Addresses given at the International Congress for Itinerant Evangelists in Amsterdam in 1986.

The Work of An Evangelist, ed. by J. D. Douglas (World Wide, 1983). Addresses given at the International Congress for Itinerant Evangelists in Amsterdam in 1983.

Thomas, Ian. *The Saving Life of Christ*, (Zondervan, 1961).

Thompson, W. Oscar, Jr. *Concentric Circles of Concern* (Broadman, 1981).

Towns, Elmer L., assisted by John Vaughan and David Siefert. *The Complete Book of Church Growth*, 2nd ed. (Tyndale, 1985).

Trotman, Dawson. *Born to Reproduce* (Back to the Bible, 1957).

Trueblood, Elton. *The Incendiary Fellowship* (Harper & Row, 1967).

_____. *The Company of the Committed* (Harper & Row, 1980).

Trumbull, Charles Gallaudet. *Taking Men Alive* (Revell, 1907).

Tuttle, Robert, Jr. *Someone Out There Needs Me* (Zondervan, 1983).

Veerman, David R. *Youth Evangelism* (Victor, 1988).

Voelkel, Jack. *Student Evangelism* (Zondervan, 1974).

Wagner, C. Peter. *Strategies for Church Growth* (Regal, 1987).

_____. *Your Church Can Grow* (Regal, 1976).

_____. *Your Church Growth, State of the Art*, ed. by Wagner, with Towns (Tyndale, 1986).

Warr, Gene. *You Can Make Disciples* (Word, 1978).

_____. *The Godly Man* (Creative Resources, 1976).

Warr, Irma. *The Godly Woman* (Creative Resources, 1976).

Warren, Richard. *Twelve Dynamic Bible Study Methods* (Victor, 1981).

Watson, David. *Called and Committed* (Harold Shaw, 1982).

_____. *I Believe in Evangelism* (Eerdmans, 1976).

Wilkins, Michael J. *Following the Master: Discipleship in the Steps of Jesus* (Zondervan, 1992).

Willard, Dallas. *The Spirit of the Disciplines* (Harper & Row, 1988).

Wilson, Carl. *With Christ in the School of Disciple Building* (Zondervan, 1976).

Wimber, John. *Power Evangelism* (Harper & Row, 1986).

Wood, A. Skevington. *Evangelism: Its Theology and Practice* (Zondervan, 1966).